DIANE SAMUELS

Diane Samuels was born in Liverpool. She now lives in London where she has been writing extensively as a dramatist and author since the early 1990s.

Kindertransport won the Verity Bargate and Meyer-Whitworth Awards, and was first produced by Soho Theatre Company in 1993. Subsequently it has been translated into many languages, performed in the West End, Off-Broadway and all over the world, and revived in 2007 in a highly acclaimed production by Shared Experience Theatre Company. Her other plays include *The True Life Fiction of Mata Hari* (Watford Palace Theatre, 2002) and *Cinderella's Daughter* (Trestle Theatre tour, 2005). She has also written widely for BBC radio, plays including *Swine*, *Doctor Y*, *Watch Out for Mister Stork* and *Hen Party*.

For younger audiences, her plays include *One Hundred Million Footsteps* (Quicksilver Theatre Company); *Chalk Circle* and *How to Beat a Giant* (Unicorn Theatre). Diane has wide experience of teaching creative writing, lecturing at the universities of Birmingham, Reading, Oxford and Goldsmiths College, London. She runs a regular writers' group and is writer-in-residence at Grafton Primary School in Islington, north London.

Diane was one of a creative team awarded a Science on Stage and Screen Award by the Wellcome Trust in 2001. The resulting work, *PUSH*, was performed at The People Show Studios in London in June 2003. Her short story, *Rope*, was one of the winners in BBC Radio 4's online short story competition, broadcast in 2002. As Pearson Creative Research Fellow 2004/5 at the British Library, she completed research into magic and her booklet *A Writer's Magic Notebook* was published in 2006. Diane regularly reviews books for the *Guardian*.

Other titles in this series

Alexi Kaye Campbell
APOLOGIA
THE FAITH MACHINE
THE PRIDE

Caryl Churchill
BLUE HEART
CHURCHILL PLAYS: THREE
CHURCHILL: SHORTS
CLOUD NINE
A DREAM PLAY *after* Strindberg
DRUNK ENOUGH TO SAY
    I LOVE YOU?
FAR AWAY
HOTEL
ICECREAM
LIGHT SHINING IN
    BUCKINGHAMSHIRE
MAD FOREST
A NUMBER
SEVEN JEWISH CHILDREN
THE SKRIKER
THIS IS A CHAIR
THYESTES *after* Seneca
TRAPS

Dominic Cooke
ARABIAN NIGHTS
NOUGHTS AND CROSSES
    after Blackman

Ariel Dorfman
DEATH AND THE MAIDEN
PURGATORIO
READER
THE RESISTANCE TRILOGY
WIDOWS

David Edgar
ALBERT SPEER
ARTHUR & GEORGE
    after Julian Barnes
CONTINENTAL DIVIDE
EDGAR: SHORTS
THE MASTER BUILDER *after* Ibsen
PENTECOST
PLAYING WITH FIRE
THE PRISONER'S DILEMMA
THE SHAPE OF THE TABLE
TESTING THE ECHO
A TIME TO KEEP *with* Stephanie Dale

Helen Edmundson
ANNA KARENINA *after* Tolstoy
THE CLEARING
CORAM BOY after Gavin
GONE TO EARTH after Webb
THE MILL ON THE FLOSS
    after Eliot
MOTHER TERESA IS DEAD
ORESTES *after* Euripides
WAR AND PEACE *after* Tolstoy

Debbie Tucker Green
BORN BAD
DIRTY BUTTERFLY
RANDOM
STONING MARY
TRADE & GENERATIONS
TRUTH AND RECONCILIATION

Mary Kelly and Maureen White
UNRAVELLING THE RIBBON

Ayub Khan-Din
EAST IS EAST
LAST DANCE AT DUM DUM
NOTES ON FALLING LEAVES
RAFTA, RAFTA...

Liz Lochhead
BLOOD AND ICE
DRACULA
EDUCATING AGNES *after* Molière
GOOD THINGS
MARY QUEEN OF SCOTS GOT HER
    HEAD CHOPPED OFF
MEDEA *after* Euripides
MISERYGUTS & TARTUFFE
    after Molière
PERFECT DAYS
THEBANS

Conor McPherson
DUBLIN CAROL
McPHERSON PLAYS: ONE
McPHERSON PLAYS: TWO
PORT AUTHORITY
THE SEAFARER
SHINING CITY
THE WEIR

Imogen Stubbs
WE HAPPY FEW

Polly Teale
AFTER MRS ROCHESTER
BRONTË
JANE EYRE *after* Brontë
MINE
SPEECHLESS *with* Linda Brogan

Amanda Whittington
BE MY BABY
LADIES' DAY
LADIES DOWN UNDER
SATIN 'N' STEEL

Nicholas Wright
CRESSIDA
HIS DARK MATERIALS *after* Pullman
MRS KLEIN
RATTIGAN'S NIJINSKY
THERESE RAQUIN *after* Zola
THE REPORTER
VINCENT IN BRIXTON
WRIGHT: FIVE PLAYS

Diane Samuels

KINDERTRANSPORT

NICK HERN BOOKS

London

www.nickhernbooks.co.uk

A Nick Hern B...

Kindertranspor... original by Nic...

Reprinted in 19... Reprinted in thi... 2010 (three tim...

Kindertranspor...

Introduction © ... Personal accou... Passages of Ge...

Diane Samuels ... of this work ...

Cover image: Eight-year-old Josepha Salmon, the first of 5,000 Jewish and non-Aryan refugees, arrives at Harwich from Germany, destined for Dovercourt Bay camp. 2nd December 1938 (Fred Morley/Hulton Archive/Getty Images)
Cover design: www.energydesignstudio.com

Typeset by Country Setting, Kingsdown, Kent CT14 8ES
Printed and bound by CPI Group (UK) Ltd, Croydon, CR0 4YY

A CIP catalogue record for this book is available from the British Library
ISBN 978 1 85459 527 0

MIX
Paper from responsible sources
FSC® C020852

Contents

Introduction

Three incidents led me to write *Kindertransport*. The first was a discussion with a close friend, in her late twenties and born into a comfortable, secure home, who described her struggle to deal with the guilt of survival. Her father had been on the Kindertransport and I was struck by how her parent's feelings had been passed down to her. The second was the experience of another friend who, at his father's funeral, overheard his mother recalling her time at Auschwitz. Until that moment he had had no idea that his mother had been in a concentration camp. The third was the ashamed admission by a fifty-five-year-old woman on a television documentary about the Kindertransport, that the feeling she felt most strongly towards her dead parents was rage at their abandonment of her, even though that abandonment had saved her life.

In 1989, I was a young mother with a one-year-old son and pregnant with my second child when I saw this TV documentary. I was struck at once by the ways in which parents and children struggled to deal with this desperate parting. I never intended to write *Kindertransport* as a modern history play. I wanted to explore the universal human experience of separation of child from parent, of refugee from the source of their culture or 'motherland'. I let this theme mull, up to my ears in nappies and baby milk, for a while longer.

In 1991, I wrote a scene between two German Jews. A mother hovers over her nine-year-old daughter and hands a new coat to the child. It is too big because it must last for 'next winter too'. She gives the girl a button and some thread and then coolly instructs her how to sew the one onto the other. By this time, my young sons were not yet one and not quite three. Artists are often drawn to the extremes of human experience in order to reflect also upon what is ordinary. 'Kinder', now in their seventies and eighties, have, on seeing the play, asked me, 'How can you possibly understand my experience so deeply?' I reply that as a young mother myself I couldn't help but be touched by what had happened to them. I was compelled to get to the heart of the dilemma. Ask a child if they would prefer to be sent away to safety if their family is in mortal danger, and he or she will, in most cases, say that they'd rather stay and die with their parents. Ask a parent what they would do in the same situation and most would say that they'd send away their child to be safe. To be a parent is to live with this hidden contradiction. I wanted to try to face it.

In 2007, when the play was revived for a national tour of the UK, my eldest son was eighteen and left home to go to university. How Life reflects Art. I found myself watching actresses in auditions read the scene in which English Evelyn loads her daughter Faith with crockery for her student flat. Then I went home and hours later loaded my boy with mugs for his student flat. I wonder at how I could understand Evelyn's suppressed heartache at Faith's departure when my children were still so young and at home with me. But many parents, from the second their child is born, know too well that here begins the road to seeing their offspring on their way. The bittersweet task is to prepare their child to manage entirely without them.

Past and present are wound around each other throughout the play. They are not distinct but inextricably connected. The re-running of what happened many years ago is not there to explain how things are now, but is a part of the inner life of the present.

I interviewed a number of the 'Kinder' as part of my research. They were all very open about their lives and feelings. Many of their actual experiences are woven into the fabric of the play. Although Eva/Evelyn and her life are fictional, most of what happens to her did happen to someone somewhere.

I used to dedicate this play to those 'Kinder' and the rest of the 10,000 who left Europe over seventy years ago. Now I see that, by entering the exceptional experience of those children who caught the trains to safety when many of them, like Eva, were too young to bear it, a crucial connection can be made with the clinging child inside us all that never wants to let go, no matter what. So, now I dedicate the play also to those fortunate children who have the opportunity to leave their parents when they are ready. And to the parents who raise their children to take that leave. No child, as Evelyn must struggle so painfully to accept, can be 'my little girl', or boy, forever, if they are to thrive.

DIANE SAMUELS
London, 2008

Thanks

Many thanks to Libby Mason; Mark Ravenhill; Jack Bradley; Abigail Morris; Soho Theatre Company; Rena Gamsa; Dawn Waterman; Naomi Fulop; Erica Burman; and particularly to Ben and Jake.

Special thanks to the 'Kinder' who were interviewed as part of research for the play: Walter Fulop; Bertha Leverton; Paula Hill; Vera Gissing and Lisa who talked at length about their journeys and their lives.

Background to the Kindertransport

The Nazi gaining of power in the 1930's signalled a huge escalation in anti-semitic activity. The first organised attack on the Jews was in April 1933 – a boycott of Jewish businesses was instigated and triggered much violence. A series of laws ensued, increasingly excluding Jews from public life. The most notorious of these were the Nuremberg Laws – the Reich Citizenship Act, depriving Jews of their citizenship, and the Act for the Protection of German Blood and German Honour. This latter law prohibited marriage or extramarital relations between 'Jews and nationals of German or allied blood' in order to ensure the survival of the German race. Later measures required that all Jewish passports were marked with the letter J – in addition Jews were banned from places of public entertainment and cultural institutions, had their driving licences revoked, their property confiscated and were often forced to live together in communal Jewish houses.

The killing of a German diplomat by a young Jew in Paris in November 1938 gave the Nazis the opportunity to engineer a huge increase in momentum. Thousands of Jewish businesses and institutions were destroyed and Jews were assaulted, killed and 30,000 herded into concentration camps. It was in response to this pogrom, known as Kristallnacht, that the Movement for the Care of Children from Germany was formed, rescuing almost 10,000 unaccompanied children, before the outbreak of war just nine months later.

Personal Accounts of the Kindertransport

I took a bus to Dovercourt where I was told help was needed at a refugee camp. This was in 1938 when the Committee for the Care of Children from Germany took over a holiday camp to act as a reception centre for Jewish refugee children.

Through this camp came children from Germany, Austria and even a few stray Sudetenlanders. At one time – when I first was there – nearly seven hundred children arrived every week, their passports altered so that all the boys were Jacob and the girls Sarah, carrying pathetic paper bags containing a few spare clothes and little else. The Germans had stripped them of everything that was worth a pfennig. The children had a big J marked on their passports so that everyone would know they were of the despised race. Their ages were at the youngest four and the oldest I remember was sixteen.

The camp was full. As many as came in had to be found places so as to allow room for the next batch. Some children went to relatives in America, many were taken in by families in Britain. Some were even sent to a settlement in Paraguay. Did they, I now wonder, ever come into contact with the Nazis who escaped from Germany and found haven there?

An impressive elderly lady, Anna Essinger – who had a school in Kent – was in charge of the camp and managed, somehow, to shape the ad hoc collection of volunteers into something of an effective organisation. It cannot have been easy: excitable young Viennese, less mercurial German ones, volunteers like myself who arrived by accident and a sprinkling of young Etonians and undergraduates meant there was plenty of energy all needing firm but diplomatic direction.

Dovercourt was important to me if only because it was an introduction to Jewish life. I got to know people there who have remained my friends ever since.

The atmosphere in the camp was highly emotional. The children old enough to understand feared what might be

happening to their relatives still in Germany: the refugee staff
knew only too well the horrors they had escaped but their
friends had not. The whole camp was charged with anxiety and
fear. It was there I first heard the word angst and appreciated
what it meant.

One evening one of the Austrian volunteers wanted to
celebrate a birthday and a half dozen others and myself went to
a local hotel for dinner. A change from camp fare where horse
meat took the place of beef was something to look forward to.
Halfway through the soup, a telephone call came from the
camp. A rumour was going round that a pogrom was under
way in Vienna: we were needed quickly to help. We rushed
back to the camp. It was impossible to describe the situation.
Imagine seven hundred contagiously frightened, crying,
wailing children milling about the huge and echoing dining
hall. The Viennese staff, poor souls, were in almost as bad a
state, anguished and caught up in total fear.

We tried to get news of what was happening in Vienna.
London apparently knew nothing. Lines to Vienna were
blocked as were those to Berlin. Finally we got a contact with
Vienna via Czechoslovakia and learned that on that occasion
the rumour was false: there was no pogrom.

Then came one of the most moving experiences of my life. It
was not going to be easy to stop what had by then become
mass hysteria. Shouting above the noise was impossible – if
anything it made matters worse. Then one of the older Jewish
helpers began to sing. First by himself, a Hebrew hymn which
everyone, even the youngest child would know. It was a hymn
which I believe had a message of hope and courage in
adversity. And the effect gradually spread until within minutes
the entire hall was filled with the sound of voices united in
song. There was something almost unearthly about such
poignant, passionate emotion. Even today, if I ever think of
that moment when from wailing the voices changed to singing,
my hair stands on end.

The winter of 1938 was a sharp one. At Dovercourt the sea
actually froze and when one night high tide and winds
combined to break the sea wall, the sea flooded into the camp
and we had to carry children through thigh-deep, very cold

water to safety. I got pneumonia for my reward and was chased into Dovercourt hospital. After a month or so I returned to the children, who by that time had moved into the old workhouse at Barham near Ipswich, a spooky place complete with cells, mortuary and graveyard.

Shortly after that the war started, no more children came in from the continent and I returned to the land.

HUGH BARRETT

a volunteer at Dovercourt – one of the major reception centres for the Kindertransport children

Freedom, liberty, human dignity, civil rights, democracy – words and phrases used in the free world to describe the rightful elements of the human condition. If however, in these recessionary times, some if not all of these ideals have a hollow ring, we can at least hope for better days to come. For we may, provided we keep within the law, say and do what we believe to be right and what we believe to be just.

Imagine, however, a society terrorised by a one-party state machinery, where none of this was possible; where the mere label Jew meant the robbing of the individual's humanity and a destiny of extermination.

Faced with this situation, our beloved parents in a spirit of total selfishness chose for us the gift of life, offered by the combined efforts of concerned Jews and Christians, fortunate to be living in the oldest democracy in the world.

Although on arrival, the path for many of us was not exactly strewn with roses, the majority worked hard – grateful for the opportunities denied to the one and a half million children who perished in the holocaust.

Former Kindertransport refugees have made their mark in every sphere of human endeavour. It is salutary to mention that the theatre in which you find yourself tonight was designed by architect Edward Mendelsohn, who came to this country on a Kindertransport in 1939.

PAULA HILL

The Kindertransport was at the centre of many episodes, which all together added up to one huge destabilising, alienating and ongoing trauma. All Jewish children in Vienna, like myself at the age of ten, were deeply aware of the terror, fear and humiliation which was all around us. And also we continuously heard our parents talking about who had been sent to Buchenwald or Dachau concentration camps; and about trying to get an affidavit from America or a visa to just about anywhere – even to unimaginable Shanghai, if one still had enough money to buy a capitalist visa.

Our family of four had already once escaped to Brussels. We overstayed our three day transit visa limit with disastrous consequences: parents separately arrested; a crack of dawn police swoop; a railway journey to a fictitious refugee camp; the shock of being pushed across the border back into Germany; arrival at Aachen railway station . . . father vanished . . . what to do next? . . . confusion, new shocks and baffling conundrums.

Back in Vienna, confidential, urgent warnings of imminent arrest from a Nazi Party friend forced my father to leave us behind and travel to London by himself, equipped with his two month business visa issued to him for the purpose of registering his photographic patent at the London Patent Office. Staying with a hardworking but poor and newly discovered uncle in the heart of the old London Docks, my father made it his first priority to find a sponsor for me and a live-in housekeeper job for my mother. Uniquely, for such a domestic job, a coveted domestic permit for entry into the country was usually granted.

The actual Kindertransport journey filled me with apprehension as well as anxiety for my mother, who, now all alone, was left behind in hostile Vienna. My brother, at his second attempt, had managed to reach Palestine on a clandestine immigrant ship. Well, in my case my mother did make it to London, to her housekeeper job, before the outbreak of war – in fact by just a few days. And yes, we were all lucky; but everything in life is at a price.

Life with my sponsors, elderly grandparents, themselves immigrants from Bessarabia at the turn of the century, with their totally different background, culture and of course

language, had its problems. This episode, followed by
evacuation to Wales and Cornwall and life there with Ethel
Maude, and her husband Jack-the-Parcel-Office, brought
yearnings of reunion with my real parents, who had themselves
been forced to live apart.

When such reunion after years of separation finally became
possible, my parents had been greatly changed by their
experiences and I had been changed beyond recognition by
mine. And I was now fifteen years old. Tragically, as a family
we were now split in two and decimated. My brother had
become rooted in the embryonic Israel. Our relatives had not
survived the Holocaust. Most sadly, neither my parents nor
myself were able to find in each other the hoped-for image we
had built up during our period of separation; and in this way
fate robbed us of the pleasure we might otherwise have had in
each other. But despite all odds, we had nevertheless survived
and it remains a perpetual mystery and wonder how, in the
midst of disaster, the seeds of recovery can remain intact.

EDWARD MENDELSOHN

Travelling to visit my grandparents in Poland as an eight-year-
old I found very exciting; snow, droskhas, sledges, halva, but
in December 1938 my mother promised me an even greater
adventure. I was to be sent to England and, what is more, she
said the Queen would be waiting for me with a bunch of
flowers on my arrival. At that time, there was little to hold me
in Hamburg, when our schooling was virtually ended, our
synagogues destroyed and where every shop, cinema,
swimming pool, theatre and sweet shop had a notice Jews
Unwanted. So, when a group of sad parents gathered at
Hamburg Hauptbahnhof to see their children off, the solemnity
of the occasion did not strike me. My mother kissed me and
left in time to wave me goodbye from the platform as our train
passed through the next station, Hamburg-Altona.

I sat in a packed compartment of children of mixed ages.
Uniformed men kept entering our compartment, but the journey
was uneventful until we crossed the Dutch border when there
was singing and jubilation. We were then shepherded aboard a

boat at the Hook of Holland bound for Harwich, arriving the following morning. We were shown into a shed, where we were all handed hard-boiled eggs and sandwiches. Some of the older boys prayed – I was ten years old and did not know how to pray, nor quite understand why. I ate my sandwiches and wondered whatever happened to the Queen.

That same night, we were taken to Butlins Holiday Camp in Lowestoft, given two blankets and a wash bowl and shown into a freezing wooden hut with two beds. I was one of about twenty who caught scarlet fever within a week and spent some six weeks in Colchester Isolation Hospital. I was then taken in by a kindly old lady in her guest house for convalescence. It was here, that on my first walk, a lady came up to me and pressed a shilling into my hand.

The ten of us were then taken to a disused Victorian workhouse called Barham House in Claydon, near Ipswich. The house had been converted to house some 800 boys and was just perfect for a ten year old – no discipline, attendance at meals was optional and it was much more fun building a raft and drifting in the nearby river. The house was a selection centre from which boys were sent to adopting parents etc. My turn came at the end of September 1939. I was adopted as a boarder by Oswestry School in Shropshire, a small public school established in 1407. Some of the tradition seemed to have changed little since, but the dormitory was absolute luxury after Barham House. The only problem was I could not speak the language, but I learned English quickly. The school provided humanity in microcosm – there was the bully, the bright, the dull, the strong, the weak. Boys who one moment beat the life out of each other in the playground only minutes later appeared in their white surplices and starched white collars singing and looking like white angels in the school chapel. The culture gap between them and myself was vast, but the gap was bridged and I emerged Head Boy six years later. I left the school feeling very much like any other school leaver, but particularly grateful for my good fortune, the opportunities given to me and the generosity and kindness shown by so many.

In 1949 my good fortune was complete when I was reunited

with my parents, who had managed to survive the war by
escaping on the last boat out of Europe to Shanghai.

SIGI FAITH

Kinderterror, Kindertransports, Kindertrauma – one sees a
chain of events linking these successive stages in the odyssey
of the children who came in 1938-39. The terror of the
children who, together with their parents, were caught up in a
modern pogrom, Kristallnacht, the night of broken glass and
broken lives, which was the true precursor of the transports.
The transports themselves, that marked the hurriedly and
sometimes frantically arranged wrench, with dimly perceived
consequences, of a child gone from his normal world and
which involved a temporary separation from a family that for
most children would last forever. And then, the trauma of re-
establishing some infrastructure of normality in a strange land,
with new families, however sympathetic and kind, with the
child enjoying a dubious status, neither a temporary guest, nor
adopted, a sort of twilight world of not knowing where he or
she belonged, which was a state of being that was to last, for
some, all their lives.

The personal tragedy of these children has now been explored
and described in numerous accounts, studies, case histories.
But the 'Kinder' also played their part on the much larger stage
of world history. In September 1938, when Chamberlain
returned from Munich waving his bit of paper, he was
undoubtedly greeted by the most rapturous and even hysterical
welcome ever accorded a British prime minister in any
circumstances, let alone one who had just negotiated what
many saw as an ignominious surrender. Less than five and a
half months later, however, the same prime minister was being
pushed by a huge groundswell of public opinion to change his
policy completely and adopt measures that put Britain on a
head-on collision course with Nazi Germany that would
ultimately lead to war. There had in fact been a sea-change in
public opinion. Traditionally, this is attributed to the occupation
of Czechoslovakia on the 15 March 1939. But, by then, the
sea-change had already taken place. What events took place

between 1 October 1938 and 15 March 1939? Only two of any note: the pogrom of Kristallnacht on 9 and 10 November, and from 10 December, the arrival of the first of the Kindertransports, which were to go on for another nine months.

One historian has described the public mood after this as a reaction to being conned. However dishonourable Munich had been perceived to be, it was meant to buy settlement, stability and peace. And what it had seemed within weeks to have produced was a pogrom and photographs on newsreels and in newspapers of unaccompanied young children carrying their pathetic suitcases and bundles of belongings, walking down gangplanks at Harwich. The reaction to this of lots of very ordinary people was one of anger and some sort of obstinate determination to bring something which would ultimately develop into the spirit of Dunkirk, Churchill and 1940. It may be some small comfort to those children, more than fifty years on, to know that that, even in some small measure, and quite unwittingly, is what they helped to bring about. But they paid, and in some cases still pay, a price.

FRED BARSCHAK

Despite the fact that I have become completely anglicised, or perhaps because of it, I do not talk readily to people (except very close friends) about my origins. I want to be thought of as completely English. Unfortunately I still cannot knit the English way, and for that reason will never knit in public. I suppose this is because I don't want to be different from real English people. I never think of my birthplace as home now and never refer to it as such.

Extract from We Came as Children, *edited by Karen Gershon and published by Macmillan London Ltd.*

Kindertransport was first performed by the Soho Theatre
Company at the Cockpit Theatre, London on 13 April 1993,
with the following cast:

RATCATCHER	Nigel Hastings
EVA	Sarah Shanson
HELGA	Ruth Mitchell
EVELYN	Elizabeth Bell
FAITH	Suzan Sylvester
LIL	Doreen Andrew

Director   Abigail Morris
Designer   Tom Piper
Lighting Designer   Mark Ridler
Music and Sound Designer   Richard Heacock

The play was subsequently performed in the United States of
America by the Manhattan Theatre Club at City Center, Stage
1, New York, in May 1994, with the following cast:

RATCATCHER	Michael Gaston
EVA	Alanna Ubach
HELGA	Jane Kaczmarek
EVELYN	Dana Ivey
FAITH	Mary Mara
LIL	Patricia Kilgarriff

Director   Abigail Morris
Scenery Designer   John Lee Beatty
Lighting Designer   Don Holder
Music and Sound Designer   Guy Sherman/Aural Fixation

Other productions in the USA include Washington DC,
Los Angeles, Philadelphia, San Francisco and San Diego.
The play has also been produced in Sweden, Germany, Austria,
Canada, Israel and Japan.

The play was revived at the Palace Theatre, Watford, on 24
May 1996, with the following cast:

RATCATCHER	Nigel Hastings
EVA	Julia Malewski
HELGA	Ruth Mitchell
EVELYN	Diana Quick
FAITH	Dido Miles
LIL	Jean Boht

Director Abigail Morris
Designer Tom Piper
Lighting Designer Jason Taylor
Music Designer Guy Sherman

This production transferred to the Vaudeville Theatre, London,
on 4 September 1996 with the same cast, except for Helga,
who was played by Sian Thomas.

The play was revived by Shared Experience Theatre Company
between March and June 2007, and toured to the Yvonne
Arnaud Theatre, Guildford; the Liverpool Playhouse; the New
Wolsey, Ipswich; Gardner Arts Centre, Brighton; the Lowry,
Salford; West Yorkshire Playhouse, Hampstead Theatre,
London; the Nuffield Theatre, Southampton and Oxford
Playhouse. The cast was as follows:

RATCATCHER	Alexi Kaye Campbell
EVA	Matti Houghton
HELGA	Pandora Colin
EVELYN	Marion Bailey
FAITH	Lily Bevan
LIL	Eileen O'Brien

Director Polly Teale
Designer Jonathan Fensom
Lighting Designer Natasha Chivers
Composer and Sound Designer Peter Salem
Movement Director Liz Ranken

KINDERTRANSPORT

For Elaine Samuels and Simon Garfield

Characters

EVELYN: *English middle-class woman. In her fifties.*

FAITH: *Evelyn's only child. In her early twenties.*

EVA: *Evelyn's younger self. She starts the play at nine years old and finishes it at seventeen years old. Jewish German becoming increasingly English.*

HELGA: *German Jewish woman of the late 1930's. In her early thirties. Eva/Evelyn's mother.*

LIL: *Eva/Evelyn's English foster mother. In her eighties.*

THE RATCATCHER: *A mythical character who also plays:* THE NAZI BORDER OFFICIAL, THE ENGLISH ORGANISER, THE POSTMAN, THE STATION GUARD.

The play takes place in a spare storage room in Evelyn's house in an outer London suburb in recent times.

ACT ONE

Scene One

Ratcatcher music.

Dusty storage room filled with crates, bags, boxes and some old furniture.

EVA, dressed in clothes of the late thirties, is sitting on the floor, reading. The book is a large, hard-backed children's story book entitled Der Rattenfänger.

HELGA, holding a coat, button, needle and thread, is nearby. She is well turned-out in clothes of the late thirties.

EVA. What's an abyss, Mutti?

HELGA (*sitting down and ushering* EVA *to sit next to her*). An abyss is a deep and terrible chasm.

EVA. What's a chasm?

HELGA. A huge gash in the rocks.

EVA. What's a . . .

    EVA *puts down the book. Music stops.*

HELGA. Eva, sew on your buttons now. Show me that you can do it.

EVA. I can't get the thread through the needle. It's too thick. You do it.

HELGA. Lick the thread . . .

EVA. Do I have to?

HELGA. Yes. Lick the thread.

EVA. I don't want to sew.

HELGA. How else will the buttons get onto the coat?

EVA. The coat's too big for me.

HELGA. It's to last next winter too.

EVA. Please.

HELGA. No.

EVA. Why won't you help me?

HELGA. You have to be able to manage on your own.

EVA. Why?

HELGA. Because you do. Now, lick the thread.

EVA *licks the thread.*

That should flatten it . . . And hold the needle firmly and place the end of the thread between your fingers . . . not too near . . . that's it . . . now try to push it through.

EVA *concentrates on the needle and thread.* HELGA *watches.*

See. You don't need me. It's good.

EVA. I don't mind having my coat open a bit. Really. I've got enough buttons.

HELGA. You'll miss it when the wind blows.

EVA. Can't I do it later.

HELGA. There's no 'later' left, Eva.

EVA. After the packing, after my story . . .

HELGA. Now.

EVA *gives in and sews.*

A key jangles in the door lock. The door opens. EVELYN *enters. She carries a tea towel. If she sees* HELGA *and* EVA, *even momentarily, she ignores them. She is followed by* FAITH.

EVELYN. Most of it is junk.

FAITH. You don't keep junk.

EVELYN. Do you want anything in particular?

FAITH. Not really.

EVELYN (*opening a box*). Pans?

FAITH. All those?

EVELYN. Are you intending to cook or eat raw?

FAITH. I was thinking of take-aways . . .

EVELYN. Have them.

> EVELYN *hands the box over to* FAITH *who receives it.*

> What else? Lights, crockery, cutlery, there's a television somewhere . . . ?

FAITH. You sound like a shop assistant trying to make a sale.

EVELYN. Just don't be a difficult customer. I told Mum we wouldn't be long. (*She opens a box and takes out a tea cup.*) Would cups and saucers be of any use?

FAITH. I prefer mugs.

EVELYN. What about for visitors?

FAITH. They can have mugs too.

EVELYN. I'll give you this set of cups and saucers just in case.

FAITH. Mum, I . . .

EVELYN. Here's a spare tea pot too.

FAITH. I don't think I need two tea pots.

EVELYN. One might break.

FAITH. You don't have to do this.

EVELYN. Who else is going to?

FAITH. Dad sent me another cheque.

EVELYN. Would you use a strainer?

FAITH. Not really.

EVELYN. Aren't you meant to save that money?

FAITH. He wouldn't mind me spending it.

EVELYN. That's not what we agreed originally.

FAITH. I'm not fourteen any more.

EVELYN. I see.

FAITH. I'd just like to buy some of my own stuff.

EVELYN. I thought you approved of my taste.

FAITH. I do. Your things are beautiful.

EVELYN. I'm glad to hear it.

FAITH. You should keep them.

EVELYN. They should be used rather than left to moulder in a box.

    EVELYN *opens a box and takes out a glass. She polishes it.*

    Glasses?

FAITH. Those must be worth a fortune.

EVELYN. Nothing is too good for my daughter.

FAITH. Might be too good for the flat.

EVELYN. You said that you and your friends were very pleased with this one.

FAITH. The rent's so high for what it is.

EVELYN (*polishing*). You said it was a bargain.

FAITH. Maybe you should have come to see it.

EVELYN. You're quite capable of choosing a place to live without my help.

    Pause.

FAITH. Maybe it's not such a good idea to move.

    EVELYN *concentrates on polishing and replacing glasses.*

    I don't feel right about it.

    EVELYN *continues to polish.*

EVELYN (*scrutinising a glass*). This is chipped.

FAITH. What do you think about waiting till I can afford to buy somewhere?

EVELYN. I think that if you say you're going, you should go.

FAITH. I can get the deposit back.

EVELYN. Like you got the deposit back last time?

FAITH. That was different.

EVELYN. It sounds remarkably similar to me.

FAITH. I'm not sure I like it.

EVELYN. Oh Faith, for heavens sakes, you're impossible.

FAITH. If you'd come to see it, you'd know.

EVELYN (*polishing madly*). How on earth did that glass get damaged. I put in enough paper.

FAITH. I don't like leaving you on your own . . .

EVELYN (*holding open another box*). Tablecloths?

FAITH *shakes her head*. EVELYN *puts them back*.

FAITH. Are you angry?

EVELYN. Absolutely not.

FAITH. Are we still friends?

EVELYN. Of course.

EVELYN *polishes*.

FAITH. I don't want to go.

EVELYN (*still polishing*). Will eleven glasses be enough?

FAITH. You can forget about the glasses.

EVELYN. You'll need something to drink from in your new home.

EVELYN *continues to polish*. FAITH, *helpless, watches*.

EVA (*sewing*). Why aren't Karla and Heinrich going on one of the trains?

HELGA. Their parents couldn't get them places.

EVA. Karla said it's because they didn't want to send them away.

HELGA. Karla says a lot of silly things.

EVA. Why's that silly?

HELGA. Of course they would send them away if they had places. Any good parent would do that.

EVA. Why?

HELGA. Because any good parent would want to protect their child.

EVA. Can't you and Vati protect me?

HELGA. Only by sending you away.

EVA. Why will I be safer with strangers?

HELGA. Your English family will be kind.

EVA. But they don't know me.

HELGA. Eva. This is for the best.

EVA. Will you miss me?

HELGA. Of course I will.

EVA. Will you write to me?

HELGA. I've told you. I will do more than miss you and write to you. Vati and I will come. We will not let you leave us behind for very long. Do you think we would really let you go if we thought that we would never see you again?

EVA. How long will it be before you come?

HELGA. Only a month or two. When the silly permits are ready.

EVA. Silly permits.

HELGA. Silly, silly permits.

EVA. The needle's stuck.

> HELGA, *with difficulty, pulls the needle through.*

Finish it off for me.

HELGA (*handing the sewing back to* EVA). No.

> EVA *takes the coat and carries on sewing.*

> EVELYN *is still polishing glasses.* FAITH *is still watching her.*

FAITH. Mum, please stop doing that.

EVELYN (*holding up the glass*). They really need washing.

> *Pause.*

> You can't stay here forever.

FAITH. Do you really want me to go?

EVELYN. What I want is irrelevant. This is your life, Faith.

FAITH. It affects you too.

EVELYN. You've made a commitment to moving into that place. Stick by it.

FAITH. It feels all wrong.

EVELYN. It seems perfectly straightforward to me.

FAITH. What do you want?

EVELYN. I want you to make a mature and reliable decision. An adult decision. This continual vacillation is not helpful to either of us.

FAITH. I can't move out yet.

> EVELYN *stops polishing.*

EVELYN. Yet?

FAITH. For a while.

EVELYN. What does that mean?

FAITH. Until after I've finished college.

EVELYN. Give it a try at least.

FAITH. I'm not going.

EVELYN. What have you got to lose?

FAITH. I'm definitely staying.

EVELYN. Are you absolutely sure?

FAITH. Absolutely.

EVELYN. So, I can't sell the house?

FAITH. No.

EVELYN. I'll have to phone the estate agent?

FAITH. Yes.

EVELYN. And say no?

FAITH. Yes.

EVELYN. How absurd.

FAITH. I'm sorry.

EVELYN. Are you intending to change your mind again?

FAITH. I don't understand why you have to go on about selling the house if I leave . . .

EVELYN. Will you or will you not change your mind?

FAITH. No.

EVELYN. Song and dance finally over?

FAITH. Yes.

   EVELYN *puts back the glass and closes the box.*

EVELYN. I expect you to keep to your word.

   She picks up the chipped glass.

FAITH. Why are you taking that?

EVELYN. A chipped glass is ruined forever.

   EVELYN *exits.* FAITH *retreats back into the attic.*

HELGA. Try to meet other Jews in England.

EVA. I will.

HELGA. They don't mind Jews there. It's like it was here when I was younger. It'll be good.

EVA. When you come, will Vati get his proper job back like he used to have?

HELGA. I'm sure he will.

EVA (*finishes sewing*). Finished.

HELGA. Now let me check the case.

HELGA *picks up a case hidden amongst the boxes and opens and checks through it.* EVA *watches her.*

FAITH *finds a trunk. She is tempted to look inside. She hesitates. She takes courage and tentatively opens it.*

(*Pulling out a dress.*) This suits you so well.

EVA. I'll only wear it for best. Promise.

HELGA (*re-folding the dress*). Someone will have to press out the creases when you get there.

FAITH (*pulling out a toy train*). Runaway train?

HELGA. The case is too full.

FAITH *makes the sound of a train whistle as she pulls pieces of train track out of the box. She starts to lay them out on the floor.*

FAITH. Runaway train went down the track
And she blew, she blew
Runaway train went down the track
And she blew, she blew
Runaway train went down the track
And blah de blah, she won't come back
And she blew, blew, blew, blew, Blew!

FAITH *continues to lay the track.*

HELGA *pulls a mouth organ out of the case.*

HELGA. What's this doing in here?

EVA. That's my mouth organ.

HELGA. You're not allowed to take anything other than clothes.

EVA. But it was my last birthday present and I'm just beginning to get the tunes right.

HELGA. The border guards will send you back to us if they find you with this. Then where will you be?

EVA. I'm sorry.

HELGA gives the mouth organ to EVA and sets to reorganising the case contents.

FAITH looks into another box. She turns it upside down. A load of dolls fall on to the floor. None of them have any clothes on. FAITH picks up a doll.

FAITH. Lucy?

She gently sits Lucy by the train set.

FAITH picks out another doll.

Gloria.

She gently sits Gloria next to Lucy and then does the same with each of the other dolls.

HELGA. There's no room for anything else. Where are your shoes?

EVA reaches over to right by FAITH's feet and gets a pair of shoes.

FAITH (*laying out another doll*). Barbara.

FAITH continues to lay out the dolls.

EVA. Here.

HELGA. Put the heel of the right shoe to your ear.

EVA. Why?

HELGA. Do it.

EVA puts the heel to her ear.

What can you hear?

EVA. It sounds like . . .

HELGA. Yes?

EVA. Ticking.

HELGA. My gold watch is in there.

EVA. How?

HELGA. The cobbler did it.

EVA. I'll look after it for you.

HELGA. And in the other heel are two rings, a chain with a Star of David and a charm bracelet for you. All made of gold.

EVA. For me?

HELGA. From my jewellery box. A travelling gift.

EVA. Thank you.

HELGA. My grandfather used to wear a black hat and coat. 'You are my children. You are my jewels.' He told me. 'We old ones invest our future in you.'

EVA *hugs* HELGA.

LIL *enters*.

LIL. You two have the quietest arguments.

FAITH. Sorry, Gran.

LIL. What for?

FAITH. Spoiling the start of your visit.

LIL. I've seen worse.

FAITH. Where is she now?

LIL. Cleaning the windows. She's begun in the sitting room.

FAITH. The cleaner came yesterday.

LIL. She's even got the step ladder out.

FAITH. What about the blue overall?

LIL. Oh yes.

FAITH. Oh God.

LIL. Lock jaw's set in.

FAITH. Don't you just love it?

LIL. Coming down?

FAITH (*looking at the toys*). I found some of my old things. I'd no idea she'd kept them.

LIL. You've made a mess, haven't you?

FAITH. Only laying them out.

LIL. You'll make your mum even worse.

FAITH. Gran, there's no harm meant.

LIL. There's harm caused all the same.

FAITH. Story of my life.

LIL. Just get this lot boxed and neaten up the room. I'll do tea.

LIL *exits*.

FAITH *reluctantly starts to put the dolls back into the box*.

HELGA *and* EVA *break their embrace*.

EVA. Listen.

HELGA. What?

EVA. I've nearly got it right.

EVA *starts to play a tune on the mouth organ. She plays well*.

EVA *finishes playing*. HELGA *applauds*.

FAITH *pulls out a small box. She opens it and looks inside*.

HELGA. Now it's time for bed.

EVA. Not yet. Let me stay up. It's my last night.

HELGA. We will carry on as we always do. Bedtime is bedtime.

EVA (*moaning*). Mutti.

HELGA. Which story do you want?

EVA. The Ratcatcher.

FAITH *pulls out a hard-backed children's story book identical to the one* HELGA *is holding*.

Pipe music.

FAITH. *Der Rattenfänger.*

HELGA. Not that one, Eva.

EVA. You said I could choose.

HELGA. Choose something else.

EVA. I don't want anything else.

HELGA *turns and picks up* EVA*'s* Rattenfänger *book.*

EVA *quickly sneaks her mouth organ into the case and closes it.*

FAITH. The Ratcatcher?

EVA. What did you say an abyss was, Mutti?

HELGA. I hope you won't ask questions like this when you're in England.

EVA. Why not?

HELGA. Listen.

HELGA *opens the book and turns its pages.*

FAITH *opens the book and flicks through it. She finds an inscription in the front of the book.*

EVA *sits close to* HELGA.

Beware little children. Take heed and learn the lesson of Hamlyn where one bad soul brought tragedy upon the whole town.

FAITH. Hamburg. 1939.

HELGA. Happy Hamlyn after the rats had been led away . . .

FAITH *carefully looks at the first page.*

. . . A town teeming with life. Full to overflowing. And every day, the good people counted their blessings. Every single one . . . Eva?

EVA. I'm listening.

FAITH (*looking at a picture*). Counting their blessings for being so lucky . . .

HELGA. They all knew how fortunate they were. All except for one very wicked soul who was ungrateful and did not count.

FAITH (*looking at another picture*). Mr Ingratitude. Jesus.

HELGA. 'We are forgotten. We are lost. We are destroyed' cried out all the uncounted blessings.

FAITH. The cloud . . .

HELGA. Then a cloud appeared in the clear, blue sky casting a shadow down below.

RATCATCHER. Who is not counting?

HELGA. Whispered the shadow.

RATCATCHER. Who has forgotten their blessings?

HELGA. It hissed.

RATCATCHER. I will find you.

HELGA. It spat.

RATCATCHER. I will search you out whoever wherever you are.

FAITH (*turning onto another page*). My God, and the shadow growing legs . . .

HELGA. ' . . . and strong arms and spiky nails . . . '

EVA. And eyes sharp as razors.

FAITH. The Ratcatcher.

The shadow of the RATCATCHER *hovers.*

A train whistle blows. Sounds of a busy railway station.

HELGA *remains stuck in bedtime story mode.* EVA *puts on her coat and hat and label with her number on it – 3362.*

HELGA. The Ratcatcher searched for the ungrateful one. He searched and searched but all in vain.

RATCATCHER. Who will make up for the lost blessings?

HELGA. He raged.

RATCATCHER. If not the one guilty soul, then all.

HELGA. And he raised an enchanted pipe to his snarling lip,
making a cruel promise to all the people of Hamlyn.

RATCATCHER. I will take the heart of your happiness away.

The RATCATCHER *plays his music.*

The sounds of the railway station become louder and louder.

Another train whistle.

EVA. Mutti! Vati! Hello! Hello! See. I did get into the carriage.
I said I would. See, I'm not crying. I said I wouldn't. I can't
open the window! It's sealed tight! Why've you taken your
gloves off? You're knocking too hard. Your knuckles are
going red! What? I can't hear you!

Sound of long, shrill train whistle.

Louder! Louder! What! I can't hear! I can't . . . I love you
too . . . See you in England.

Sounds of train starting to move. EVA *sits.*

I mustn't stare at that cross-eyed boy.

Train whistle blows.

What if he talks to me?

The train moves faster.

I'll have to pretend I can't hear him.

The train is well on its way.

There's no point in crying.

The RATCATCHER *music weaves around the train's
chugging.*

We'll see our Muttis and Vatis soon enough.

*The music seems to take on the melody of a familiar play-
tune.* EVA *tunes in to it and sings.*

Hoppe, hoppe Reiter
Wenn er fällt dann schreit er
Fällt er in den Graben
Fressen ihn die Raben
Fällt er in den Sumpf
Macht der Reiter plumps.

(*Hop hop hop hop rider / Do not fall beside her / If into the ditch you fall / The Ratman gets you all / And don't have the desire / To fall into the mire.*)

We're all going to England, to England, to England . . .

The train slows down and stops.

In England all the men have pipes and look like Sherlock Holmes and everybody has a dog.

Enter a Nazi BORDER OFFICIAL. *He approaches* EVA.

FAITH *watches*.

OFFICER. No councillor in here?

EVA. She's in the next carriage.

OFFICER (*picking up* EVA*'s case*). Whose case is this?

EVA. Mine.

OFFICER. Stand up straight.

EVA *stands*.

OFFICER. Turn your label round then. It's gone the wrong way. Can't see your number.

EVA (*turning the label round. Quietly*). Sorry.

OFFICER. Speak up.

EVA. Sorry.

OFFICER. Sir! Sorry, Sir.

EVA. Sorry, Sir.

OFFICER. No one will know what to do with you if they can't see your number.

Silence.

Will they?

EVA. No, Sir.

OFFICER. Might have to remove you from the train.

Silence.

Mightn't we?

EVA. Yes, Sir.

OFFICER. D'you know it at least?

EVA. Pardon, Sir?

OFFICER. Know your number. If you don't know it you might forget who you are.

EVA. 3362, Sir.

OFFICER (*taking out a pen*). Don't want you to forget who you are now, do we?

EVA. No, Sir.

OFFICER. Let me remind you.

He draws a huge star of David on the label.

There. That should tell 'em wherever it is you're going. Best to keep them informed, eh?

EVA (*terrified*). Yes, Sir.

OFFICER *opens and searches the case, throwing everything onto the floor. He finds the mouth organ.*

OFFICER. You can't take valuables out of the country. Can't take anything for gain.

EVA. I wouldn't sell it, Sir.

OFFICER. What's it for then?

EVA. For music, Sir. I play it, Sir.

OFFICER. You any good?

EVA. I suppose so . . .

OFFICER. Go on then. Prove it's not just to make money.

EVA *takes it and plays nervously, badly.*

You need more practice. Better keep it.

OFFICER *bodysearches* EVA.

What money have you got?

OFFICER *digs into* EVA*'s pockets and takes out a few coins which he takes and pockets.*

Better clear up the mess.

EVA *starts to clear up.*

OFFICER *feels in a pocket and produces a toffee. He gives the toffee to* EVA.

Here kiddie. A sweetie for you.

OFFICER *ruffles* EVA*'s hair and exits.*

EVA *grips the toffee tightly and tidies up the clothes into the case.*

The train starts up again and moves faster and faster.

EVA. The border! It's the border! Yes! We're out! Out! Stuff your stupid Hitler. Stuff your stupid toffees! (S*he throws down the toffee*). Keep them! Hope your eyes fall out and you die the worst death on earth! Hope no one buries you! Hope the rats come and eat up all your remains until there's nothing left!

Sounds of the train stopping again. The music becomes lighter. EVA *eats and drinks greedily.*

We can really have as many cakes as we want. That Dutch lady said. And sweets. And lemonade. I'm going to stuff my pockets for later. Who says it's naughty? They all want us to be happy, don't they? That's exactly what I'm doing. Making myself very, very happy.

Sound of a ship's horn and the lapping of waves.

If you lick your lips you'll taste the salt. Sea salt.

She starts to cough as if holding down the goodies she has just guzzled. She recovers her composure.

I don't know why they call it the Hook of Holland. It's nothing like one. Look at it. How's that a hook? (*Coughing*.) . . . it won't come . . . nothing will come out of me.

EVA *coughs and coughs. Sound of a ship's horn*.

(*Weakened by the journey and the coughing*.) Is this actually England? Is it?

EVA *readies herself and tentatively steps forward*.

How can you just go through like that? Don't they search you?

EVA *stops and bends down suddenly*.

(*Picking up one penny*.) A penny? They have such big money here. It must be a sign of good luck.

EVA *pockets the penny*. RATCATCHER*'s music*.

HELGA. In the piper's wake they skipped. All the children up the mountain, on and on till . . . crash. With a roar the rock opened, the music stopped, and the children disappeared into the abyss.

FAITH (*reading*). 'Strasse ohne Trommeln'. (*'Drumless street.'*)

HELGA. And the weeping people renamed the street where the children had last been seen, 'Drumless street'. A hollow highway where music was forbidden. Then they chiselled into the walls of Hamlyn the tragic tale of the lost kinder who left in the summer of 1284 and were never seen thereafter.

FAITH *starts to play a discordant tune on the mouth organ*.

Blackout.

Scene Two

HELGA *has gone.*

FAITH *has settled down to read a letter from the box.*

EVA *has taken her coat off. Her case is by her feet. She has a tin mug of tea in one hand and a piece of bread in the other.*

Railway station sounds. A train announcement in English.

EVA (*trying to put on a brave face*). I am very lucky. I appreciate all of this, really I do, Mutti.

She takes a bite out of the bread.

FAITH (*reading*). 'March 6th, 1941.'

EVA. I'm glad to be eating the bread of freedom even if it does taste like sponge buttered with greasy salt.

She sips the tea.

FAITH. 'Dearest Eva, little Eva who must now be so big.'

EVA. How good it is to sip the tea of England even if it does taste like dishwater. I am so fortunate not to be at home with you and Vati. How good it is to have escaped.

FAITH. 'See, I write you in English for sure am I that it now is your best language.'

EVA. If I could, if it wasn't ungrateful, I'd wish that they hadn't made this 'stuff' for me so I had to drink and eat it; wish that the houses I saw on the way here weren't all the same, red-brick squares so I could look forward to living somewhere like our house, elegant; wish they all spoke German.

EVA *sighs and takes another sip.*

FAITH. 'Tantchen Marianne send her love. She is not too well at present as her chest is very bad. It does not help that we have poor heating here in the small flat that Vati and me now share with her.'

EVA. Mind you, Mutti, it was wonderful going on the red bus. We went right through London. I sat on the top. I could see everything. Upstairs on a bus. It's unbelievable!

FAITH. 'Are you keeping up your good studies at school and working as hard and well as always you did? Also we hope that you be a good girl for the Mr and Mrs Miller. Vati wants me to tell you that he is well and his spirits are up. Life is not so bad. We are happy enough.'

An English ORGANISER *enters.*

EVA (*standing up and bowing. Very carefully pronouncing*). Good bye to you.

ORGANISER. What you on about?

EVA. About?

ORGANISER. Never mind. Is your name Eva (*Pauses to work out the pronunciation.*) Schlesinger?

EVA *looks uncertain.*

How d'you say it? EEvaa Shshlezzinnjerr?

EVA (*different pronunciation*). Eva Schlesinger?

ORGANISER. Yes. (*Points at her.*) You?

EVA. Schlesinger Eva.

ORGANISER. You are she?

EVA. Ich? (*Me?*)

ORGANISER. Eva?

EVA. Jawohl, mein Herr. (*Yes, sir.*)

ORGANISER. It appears that your English family have been delayed.

EVA. Ich verstehe nicht, mein Herr. (*I don't understand, sir.*)

ORGANISER (*miming with hands and talking very slowly*). Your . . . English Mother . . . Mutter?

EVA. Mutter.

ORGANISER (*miming graphically*). Not coming yet!

EVA. Niemand kommt? (*No one's coming to meet me?*)

ORGANISER (*nodding*). That's right.

EVA. Niemand? (*No one at all?*)

ORGANISER (*nodding*). That's right.

EVA. Aber meine Mutter hat gesagt, dass ich eine englische Familie habe. (*But my mother said that I had a family here.*)

EVA *starts crying*.

ORGANISER. What is it about me that gets them all crying?

EVA. Ich will meine Mutti. Ich will meinen Vati. (*I want my mum. I want my dad.*)

ORGANISER. I'm sorry, love. I can't understand a word you're saying.

EVA. Wer wird für mich sorgen? (*Who will look after me?*)

ORGANISER. She'll be here soon.

EVA. Wohin soll ich gehen? (*Where will I go?*)

ORGANISER. You've just got to wait.

EVA. Bitte, schicken Sie mich nicht nach Deutschland zurück. (*Please don't send me back to Germany.*)

ORGANISER. It's not the end of the world.

EVA *sniffs*.

(*Taking a hankie out of his pocket.*) Here.

EVA *hesitates*.

I've not used it.

EVA *takes it, wipes her eyes and blows her nose*.

I should really leave you to use your sleeve like most of the others are doing.

EVA (*holding out the hankie to return it*). Entschuldigung. Es ist jetzt ein bisschen schmutzig. (*I'm sorry. I've made it a bit dirty.*)

ORGANISER (*taking the hankie*). I just can't stand it when you all start crying.

EVA. Werden Sie für mich sorgen? (*Will you look after me?*)

ORGANISER. At least you've stopped now. Right. I'd better go and do that lot over there.

> ORGANISER *makes to exit.* EVA *makes to follow him.*

No. No. You stay where you are.

> EVA *looks perplexed.*

(*Barking at her as if to a dog.*) Sit!

> EVA *looks at the chair and returns to it.*

Stay!

> ORGANISER *exits.*

FAITH (*still reading*). Remember that we always love and think of you. Always. No matter what. Mutti.

> FAITH *starts to play the mouth organ.*

EVA (*listening to the heel of her shoe*). Yes. It is. It's ticking.

> She tries to twist the heel.

I need to know the time. Come on.

> She twists again with much more effort. Nothing shifts. She holds the heel to her ear and shakes it.

My gold rings. I want to try on my new rings.

> She takes off the other shoe.

My chain. I can wear it now. For the first time I can wear it out on top of my clothes.

> She thwacks the heels against the side of the chair.

Mutti, you were right about Herr Reichman. He is a very reliable cobbler who doesn't know how to make a faulty shoe. He's locked in my keepsakes. I'll never get them now. (*Putting the shoe back on.*) They'll just be there in my shoes, jangling and ticking away, with me walking on them for ever and ever. What good's a watch when you can't see its face.

LIL *enters.*

FAITH. I will put the things away . . .

LIL. You said that before.

FAITH. I'm just about to.

LIL. What about tea?

FAITH. I don't want any.

EVA (*standing up*). Goodbye to you.

LIL (*to* EVA). Poor lamb. You must be exhausted. Scared as well probably. Last thing you need is me being late.

EVA *stands and bows.*

EVA. Goodbye to you.

LIL. Goodbye?

EVA. Goodbye.

LIL. Who taught you English? German teacher was it? (*Holds out her hand.*) Hello.

EVA *holds out her hand.*

LIL (*shaking* EVA's *hand*). Hello.

EVA (*carefully*). Hello.

LIL (*speaking slowly*). My name is Mrs Miller. Lil Miller.

EVA. Angenehm. (*I'm pleased to meet you.*)

LIL. I'm sorry, love. Don't speak German. You'll have to learn English.

Points to EVA's *case and gestures 'out'.*

Set to go then?

EVA *picks up her case, puts on her coat and stands ready.*

LIL (*pointing at the label with the number and Star of David on it*). What's this?

EVA. Ich muss es tragen. Ich hasse es. (*I have to wear it. I hate it.*)

LIL. Why don't we get rid of it?

EVA *hesitates.*

LIL. You don't need it on now I've come.

EVA. Und wenn ich meine Nummer vergesse? (*What if I forget my number?*)

LIL *takes the label off.*

LIL. All gone.

EVA. Sind Sie sicher? (*Can you do that?*)

LIL (*gesturing*). Over. Finished. Done. Goodbye. Yes. That's the word. Goodbye.

EVA. Ich verstehe. (*I understand.*)

LIL *takes her hand.*

LIL. I like you. Come on. Better get to Manchester now. D'you like singing?

LIL *sings a snatch of 'Runaway Train'.*

Sit down there. And don't put your feet on the seats. Doing alright?

LIL *takes out a packet of cigarettes and starts to light up.*

EVA *looks horrified.*

EVA. Sie sollten nicht rauchen. Das ist schrecklich. (*You can't smoke. It's a dirty habit.*)

LIL. Don't you like smoking?

EVA. Nur gewöhnliche Leute rauchen. (*Only common people smoke.*)

LIL. You'll just have to get used to it.

EVA. Das macht die Finger gelb und knochig. (*It makes your fingers go yellow and boney.*)

LIL. What you on about? Look. (*She takes out a cigarette.*) This is a cigarette. I light it. (*She lights it.*) I smoke it. (*She takes a drag.*) Oh, that's good. And I enjoy it. You'll have to learn to go down the shops and get my twenty Players for me.

EVA. Wie ist das wenn man raucht? (*What's it like when you smoke?*)

LIL. That can be the first English you learn.

EVA (*pointing at the cigarette*). Darf ich? (*Can I have a go?*)

LIL. Didn't your mam ever tell you that's it's bad for children to smoke?

EVA. Bitte. (*Please.*)

LIL. You're a naughty girl, you.

EVA. Nur einmal. (*Just one try.*)

LIL (*holding the cigarette out to her*). A quickie then.

EVA *draws on the cigarette. She likes it.*

Away from home, out in the world two minutes and already you're smoking like a chimney.

EVA. I have hunger.

LIL. Should have said before. (*Looking at her watch.*) Alright. Wait there!

LIL *rushes off.*

EVA. Frau Lil! Frau Lil! Verlassen Sie mich nicht! Ich habe nicht einmal eine Fahrkarte! Kommen Sie bitte zurück! (*Frau Lil! Frau Lil! Don't leave me! I don't even have my ticket! Please come back!*)

EVA *looks around desperately.*

The whistle blows.

Hilfe! Hilfe! Niemand sorgt für mich! (*Help! Help! No one's looking after me!*).

LIL *rushes in holding a large piece of cake.*

LIL. Stop fretting and eat your Madeira cake.

She gives the cake to EVA *who eats it hungrily.*

FAITH. I don't want any tea.

LIL. Don't make me have it on my own.

FAITH. What about Mum?

LIL. She's polishing furniture.

FAITH. Has she had the vacuum out yet?

LIL. Stop it.

FAITH. I'm sorry. I'm not hungry.

LIL (*signalling at the mess*). Get on with it, Faith.

FAITH. Gran . . .

LIL. Now.

FAITH. If you don't mind, I'm just looking . . .

LIL (*bending down to pick things up*). Time to come out and face the music.

FAITH. Look what I've found . . .

FAITH *pulls out the* Rattenfänger *book.*

LIL. Stop poking about, will you.

FAITH. It's the Ratcatcher story. I didn't know we had a copy.

LIL. What Ratcatcher story?

FAITH. You know, 'The Ratcatcher ever-ready in the shadows'.

LIL. Don't recall it.

FAITH. Yes you do. All the parents say, 'If you're not good the Ratcatcher will come and get you.' But the children don't listen. And he comes out of the dark night with his spiky nails and razor eyes and tempts them with sweets. And they're so naughty that they follow him into the abyss.

LIL. Why d'you think I know it?

FAITH. Mum used to tell me. She said she was told it when she was little.

LIL. She must have read it herself.

FAITH. She can't have done. Not from this book. It's in German.

LIL. Let me see.

LIL *takes the book and opens it.*

Where did you get this?

FAITH. That box.

LIL *looks in the box at the letters and photos.*

Did it belong to the little Jewish girl you had staying with you during the war?

LIL. What d'you mean?

FAITH *picks up a photo and shows it to* LIL.

FAITH. Eva something.

LIL. How d'you know about this Eva?

FAITH. I read some stuff.

LIL. What have you read?

FAITH. Letters from her parents, bits from her diary . . .

LIL. You should leave things alone.

FAITH. D'you know why Mum's got all her belongings?

LIL. No idea.

FAITH. I'm surprised you've never mentioned her.

LIL. A million things happened during the war.

FAITH. Were you close?

LIL. She wasn't with us for long.

FAITH. It must have been for at least two years . . .

LIL. Was it?

FAITH. Why are you being so cagey?

LIL. I'm hungry for my tea.

FAITH (*joking*). Did you kill her and try to hide the evidence?

LIL. Don't be so bloody stupid!

FAITH. Gran?

LIL. I didn't think that your mother had kept anything from that time.

FAITH. It's upset you, hasn't it?

LIL. I don't know why.

FAITH. Did something bad happen to her?

LIL. To who?

FAITH (*holding up the photo*). Little Eva.

LIL. No. No. She's alright.

FAITH. D'you know where she is?

LIL. Stop going on at me will you.

FAITH. It's ok. Sorry. Don't worry. I'll ask Mum.

LIL. No. Don't. Don't you dare.

FAITH. Why not?

LIL. Just leave it.

FAITH. Why?

   LIL *is silent*.

   What?

LIL. Give me that photo.

FAITH. Why should I?

LIL. Those are your mother's private possessions, Faith.

   FAITH *pulls back and looks at the photo closely*.

   LIL *holds out her hand for it*.

FAITH *keeps hold*.

FAITH. No they're not. They really belong to that Eva . . .

LIL *keeps holding out her hand*.

LIL. Your mother's things.

FAITH. Who is this little girl?

LIL. Faith.

FAITH. Who?

LIL *looks down*.

Is she something to do with Mum?

LIL. Faith.

FAITH. Is she?

LIL. You shouldn't have looked at them.

FAITH. Is she Mum?

LIL. Put them away now.

FAITH. Shit.

LIL. Put them away.

FAITH. You told me she was three days old when she came to you.

LIL. What am I meant to say?

FAITH. Just answer.

LIL. She was nine years when she came.

FAITH. And she was called Eva?

LIL. I'm not going to lie.

FAITH. And she spoke German and wore a yellow star?

LIL. There was no yellow star.

FAITH. But she was Jewish?

LIL. It was a long time ago.

FAITH. This is unbelievable.

LIL. You really shouldn't have looked.

FAITH. I've asked you both so many times about her real family.

LIL. Aren't I real now?

FAITH. Did you ever meet her parents?

LIL. No.

FAITH. Do you know what happened to them?

LIL. They died.

FAITH. Why make a secret out of it?

LIL. She just wanted to put the past behind her. It was for the best.

FAITH. Whose best?

LIL. Hers.

FAITH. What about mine?

LIL. Don't be so bloody selfish.

FAITH. Don't you think that this affects me?

LIL. It affects her more.

FAITH. I know nothing about her.

LIL. She's still your mam, Faith. Don't make a big deal out of something that was over and done with before you were born.

FAITH. What was the point in having me if she was going to cut herself off?

EVA, *pen and paper in hand, sits on the other side of* LIL.

EVA (*showing the letter to* LIL). My letter is finished.

LIL. Is it now?

EVA. At the hour of lunch I did it. I have help from teacher. She said it to be in mine words. She put some English in.

LIL. Show me.

> EVA *gives the letter to* LIL.

> (*Reading the letter out loud.*) 'Sirs, I am nine years old and now have come to live my days in Manchester with a very kind lady and her family by the name of Miller.'

EVA (*taking over the reading*). 'My Mother and Father, Helga and Werner Schlesinger, are not come with me because they would be illegal to do so. But I am much sad that they must to be in Hamburg in Germany because there are dangers in that place for them in that they are Jewish people. It is in your powers to give them permit that they come into England. Please will you give it to them. Job will be here for them I make sure of it. I remain yours faithfully, Eva Schlesinger.'

LIL. This is good. You write English better than our Nora and she's been speaking it all her life.

EVA. I did all the lunchtime.

LIL. What about your sandwiches?

EVA. Got ham in. I not to eat ham. It from pig.

LIL. But I asked you and you said yes.

EVA. Then I think good to eat it looked.

LIL. It is good. Special treat for us all.

EVA. But Mutti I think see me and not be pleased. So not eat. God not like. This is law of Jews.

LIL. Look, love, if it's God you're worried about, the Lord Jesus said that we needn't keep to the old laws any more. They had their day years ago.

EVA. Did they?

LIL. Course they did. Made for olden times. New things have come to put in their place.

EVA. For all persons? Even Jews?

LIL. Especially for Jews.

EVA. Why not all Jews think that?

LIL. Hanging on to the past, I suppose. Now, listen you.
    Always make time to eat. Always. There's enough starving
    children in the world without adding to their number.

EVA. Please. You do letter.

LIL. Got a lot to do before I can do that. Need to find them
    jobs. Sort out sponsors. We'll put an ad in the paper.
    (*Picking up a newspaper.*) Here's the sort of thing.
    (*Reading.*) 'Married couple, still in Vienna; speak excellent
    English; want position. Wife perfect cook; husband
    experienced driver. Write to etc . . . ' Got to word it right.

EVA. Vati is in bank. We write he to be in bank.

LIL. Can't do that love.

EVA. But he do that. He master in bank. Nazis stop him. Here
    he do again. No Nazis here.

LIL. The only jobs they'll let them do is as servants. I checked.
    What about gardener?

EVA. Father? No. At home, Herr Kuttel gardener.

LIL. Well, what about cook then?

EVA. Mutti know to cook, I think.

LIL. Cook. Good. And we'll say she can clean. Plus their
    English is fluent. What about your dad as a butler?

EVA. They not servants!

LIL. Do you want them here as servants or over there?

EVA. If not do servant, they not come?

LIL. No. Simple as that.

EVA. Alright. Father could do butler.

LIL. Used to be a bank manager didn't he? Stand the same
    way do butlers and bank managers.

EVA. Stand same way?

LIL. Like this.

LIL *stands in formal, stiff, straight-backed pose.*

LIL. Butler. (*She poses.*) Bank manager. (*She poses.*) Same thing.

EVA. Not in Germany.

LIL. Different sense of humour too.

EVA. Sense . . .

LIL. Joke, lovie. Just a joke.

EVA. We call you Laugh A Minute.

LIL (*chuffed and taken aback*). Where d'you learn that?

EVA. Please do ad now.

LIL (*reading paper*). 'Married couple. Non-Aryan. Very cultured.' We'll copy this.

EVA *takes paper off her and pores over it.*

FAITH (*looking at a photo*). She must have changed a lot.

LIL. She had to cope with a lot.

FAITH. What exactly?

LIL. Losing her parents like that.

FAITH. Like what?

LIL. Coming over on her own . . .

FAITH. Why on her own?

LIL. They only had children on those trains.

FAITH. Why did you take her?

LIL. I wanted to help.

FAITH. But when . . . ?

LIL. You mustn't tell your mother I told you . . .

FAITH. When exactly did she come?

LIL. She arrived on January 7th, 1939.

FAITH. On her birthday.

LIL. It wasn't her birthday then.

FAITH. What d'you mean?

LIL. She changed her birthday. When she was sixteen. She changed it to the day I first picked her up from the station. Promise me you won't tell her, Faith.

FAITH. When's her real birthday?

LIL. Can't recall.

FAITH. But January 7th is on her passport. How could she get away with that?

LIL. She made sure it went onto all the naturalisation papers. She said they'd made a mistake on the papers she came in on.

FAITH. Is that when she changed her name too?

LIL. Yes.

FAITH. Why?

LIL. She just wanted to make a fresh start.

FAITH. So what else did she change?

EVA *sneaks in front of them, trying not to be seen by* LIL.

EVA *goes very quiet. Her head droops.*

LIL. You talk first.

EVA. About what?

LIL. Lying.

EVA. I not know . . .

LIL. Yes you do. Where have you been?

EVA. Ich bin verantwortlich. Ich muss es machen. (*It's all up to me. I have to.*)

LIL. Not the German, Eva.

EVA. Ich muss sie befreien. Ich muss sie befreien. (*I have to get them out. There's no one else.*)

LIL. Don't hide behind the German. It won't protect you and you know it.

EVA. Du darfst mich nicht hindern. Du darfst nicht! (*You mustn't try to stop me. You mustn't.*)

LIL. In English! English!

EVA. Nicht englisch! Deutsch! Ich bin Deutsche! (*Not English! German! I'm German!*)

LIL. I've had enough of this, you little snake! Bloody stop it!

EVA (*sobbing*). No good. No good.

LIL. Cut out the snivels! Now! I want facts from you! True ones! Where've you been!

EVA. English lesson.

LIL. How long for?

EVA. Two hours.

LIL. It's half past six now.

EVA. Walk home slow.

LIL. You're not learning English.

EVA. You not like . . .

LIL. If there's one thing I cannot stand, it's a little liar! Where've you been!

EVA. Please . . .

LIL. Now! Before I chuck you out and never let you back in!

EVA. I can't.

LIL. You bloody well better had!

EVA. Promise not stop me.

LIL. No promises. Truth.

EVA. Please . . .

LIL. Now!

EVA. Out walking.

LIL. Where?

EVA. Streets. Knocking on doors.

LIL. What doors?

EVA. Big houses. Rich people.

LIL. Eva!

EVA. I say about (*Pronouncing very carefully.*) Butler and
  Housekeeper and Chauffeur and Gardener.

LIL. And what do they say?

EVA. 'We have already got.' Or some want to give tea and be
  sorry. Gentleman gave money at me.

LIL. The shame of it. What on earth d'you think we put an ad
  in for! To pass the time and have a laugh?

EVA. Sorry.

LIL. Don't you trust me! What good is it if you don't bloody
  trust me.

EVA. Sorry.

LIL. I took you in didn't I! Said I'd look after you! Why'd you
  throw it back in my face! Walking the streets like some
  begging little orphan!

EVA. Do not throw me out. Please.

LIL. Of course, I'm not going to throw you out!

EVA. Please. Nowhere else to go.

LIL (*gentler*). Of course, I'm not going to throw you out.

EVA. Even if I'm naughty.

LIL. Not even if you're naughty.

  LIL *hugs* EVA.

EVA. Want to be with them.

LIL. You can't be. Not now.

EVA. When?

LIL. Sooner or later.

EVA. I have to get permits.

LIL. Just be glad you're safe.

EVA. What good me to be safe?

LIL. Better than no one being safe, isn't it?

EVA. I must to help . . .

LIL. You are doing.

EVA. But jobs . . .

LIL. . . . are being found for them.

> EVA *drops her head*.

> Be a bit patient won't you?

> EVA *shrugs*.

> Cheer up and give them out there good reason to be happy. Else what've they got to smile for?

> EVA *shrugs*.

> Well. What've they got?

EVA (*quietly. German*). Nichts.

LIL. What's that?

EVA (*louder. German*). Nichts. Nothing.

LIL. That's right, little getaway. Nothing.

> EVA *exits*.

FAITH. Did Dad know about this?

LIL. Don't go telling him.

FAITH. He must have had some idea.

LIL. He had no reason to know any more than you did.

> *The door opens*. EVELYN *enters*.

EVELYN. There's a beautifully laid table with a cold pot of tea on it in the kitchen.

LIL. We got waylaid.

EVELYN. Why are you both still in here? Come on out and I'll lock the door.

FAITH *does not move*.

LIL (*to* EVELYN). You go down. I'm just getting something sorted.

EVELYN. Can't you do that elsewhere?

EVELYN *sees the toys*.

Oh Faith, what on earth have you been doing?

EVELYN *starts to tidy up the dolls*.

LIL. I told her to put them away.

EVELYN. It's probably far better if I deal with it.

LIL. Don't bother yourself, love.

EVELYN. You two go down.

FAITH. Why did you keep those dolls?

EVELYN. I'm sorry?

FAITH. You used to throw them in the bin as if they were rubbish.

EVELYN. I hardly think so, darling.

FAITH. I remember.

EVELYN. Maybe once when you'd made a terrible mess.

FAITH. You did it all the time. I never expected to find them up here. I always thought you must have thrown them all away for good.

EVELYN. I wouldn't do that.

FAITH. I found a box of letters and photographs.

LIL. Let's boil up a fresh kettle.

FAITH. I don't want any tea.

LIL. Faith.

FAITH. How can I pretend that nothing has happened?

EVELYN. Darling, you really do not need to get so distressed about the smallest thing.

LIL. I'll put them away . . .

EVELYN. No, Mum, please. I'd much rather do it myself.

FAITH. I found this book too.

LIL. Watch yourself.

EVELYN *tidies up*.

FAITH. Would you like to see the book?

EVELYN. We'd better have tea soon or it'll be time for dinner.

FAITH. You remember the story of the Ratcatcher, don't you? This must be your book. It's not at all like I imagined. It's in German.

LIL. No more, Faith.

FAITH. Mum, tell me about Eva Schlesinger.

EVELYN (*to* LIL). What have people been saying?

LIL (*to* EVELYN). Don't look at me.

EVELYN. Will you please put that book back where you found it.

FAITH. Talk to me.

EVELYN. There is nothing to talk about.

FAITH. Please tell me the truth about yourself.

EVELYN (*turning to* LIL). Mum?

LIL (*to* FAITH). You shouldn't have brought it up.

FAITH. I can't un-know it.

EVELYN. Whatever it is you think you've discovered. You must forget it.

FAITH. Of course I can't forget it.

EVELYN. I certainly have.

FAITH. You do admit that you were Eva Schlesinger then?

EVELYN. No I didn't . . . Did I? . . . No . . .

    EVELYN *goes blank*.

FAITH. Mum?

EVELYN (*to* LIL). Why can't she respect my privacy?

LIL. I told her that she shouldn't have looked.

FAITH. I don't see why not.

LIL (*to* FAITH). Why can't you give over sometimes.

EVELYN. It's perfectly alright.

FAITH. Are you ok, Mum?

EVELYN. We'll all agree to let it be.

FAITH. What do you mean?

EVELYN (*looking at the papers and photos*). Mum, would you mind putting them all away?

LIL (*clearing up*). I don't know why you had to hold onto it all anyway.

EVELYN. They need sifting. I never could . . . There's some documents in there . . . I have to keep those . . . the rest needed throwing away years ago.

FAITH. You mustn't throw them away. Let me have them.

EVELYN (*to* FAITH). I don't want you getting involved with all that. No. (*To* Lil). She mustn't. It's got nothing to do with her.

FAITH. It has got something to do with me.

EVELYN. It has got nothing to do with you at all.

FAITH. I want to know about you.

EVELYN. You do know about me.

FAITH. And my grandparents.

LIL (*to* EVELYN). You'll have to talk to her.

EVELYN. I think, Faith, that this conversation must come to a close.

FAITH. Don't do this, Mother. You always do this. It only makes things worse.

EVELYN. We cannot continue to discuss the subject profitably.

EVELYN *makes to exit*.

LIL. You can't leave it like this, Evelyn.

FAITH *leaps in front of her and bars the door*.

FAITH. I'm not letting it go.

EVELYN. What is wrong with you?

FAITH. Do you have any idea what it's like having a mother who walks out on you the moment you begin to disagree with her? Who polishes and cleans like a maniac?

EVELYN. Pull yourself together.

FAITH. Pull myself together? You're so paranoid you go stiff at every speck of dust or object out of place in your precious home . . .

EVELYN. I care about where I live. I know what it's worth.

FAITH. You can't go on a train without hyper-ventilating. You cross the road if you see a policeman or traffic warden.

EVELYN. How ridiculous.

FAITH. I've watched your panic attacks. All that shaking and gulping like you're going to die. But always it's me who's getting things out of proportion because I get scared by them.

EVELYN. Look at you now.

FAITH. I have never been a good enough daughter.

EVELYN. What are you talking about?

FAITH. I've always thought it was my fault that you were so unhappy.

EVELYN. I am not unhappy. Heavens knows why you are.

FAITH. Because of you.

EVELYN. Don't talk such nonsense.

FAITH. Because all you've given me is a pack of lies.

LIL. Watch what you say, Faith.

EVELYN. I have never lied to you.

FAITH. Don't try making out I'm making this up. I've got proof. Look. Evidence.

EVELYN. You're hysterical.

EVELYN *tries to leave again.* FAITH *continues to block her way.*

FAITH. Jesus. How could I possibly not be a bad child with such a terrible mother!

LIL. That's enough.

FAITH. A fucking, awful, lying cow of a mother.

EVELYN. How dare you.

LIL. You don't know the half of it, madam.

EVELYN. Have you finished?

FAITH. Why did you never explain about yourself?

EVELYN. Have you quite finished?

FAITH. I could kill you.

LIL (*going for* FAITH). I'll bloody kill you first!

FAITH *runs away.* LIL *follows her.*

Pipe music. The shadow of the RATCATCHER *looms.*

EVA. He's coming.

EVELYN. Stop.

EVA. His eyes are sharp as knives.

EVELYN. Be quiet.

EVA. He'll cut off my nose.

EVELYN. He's not coming.

EVA. He'll burn my fingers till they melt.

EVELYN. You've not done anything wrong.

EVA. He'll pull out my hair one piece at a time.

EVELYN. You're a good girl.

EVA. Don't let him come. Please!

EVELYN. He won't come.

EVA. He will.

EVELYN. I promise. I won't let him. I'll do everything I can to stop him. You'll see. You're with me now. He can't touch me. Do you understand? I'm here. You're being looked after. I won't go away. I'll make it all disappear. I'll get rid of him. He won't take you anywhere ever again.

End of Act One.

ACT TWO

Scene One

The room is dim. The air is stale and smoke-filled.

EVELYN'*s clothes and hair are unkempt. Beside her is an ashtray containing a large number of cigarette stubs.*

Around her sit HELGA *with the* Rattenfänger *book and a curled-up* EVA.

HELGA (*to* EVA). Do you understand what I mean about your being my jewels?

EVA. That's not in the story.

HELGA. Do you understand?

EVA. Sort of.

HELGA. We all die one day, but jewels never fade or perish. Through our children we live. That's how we cheat death.

EVA. You're not going to die are you?

HELGA. Not yet.

EVA. Not for a long time.

HELGA. I hope not.

EVA. Promise me.

HELGA. Promise me you'll be a good girl in England.

EVA. I promise.

A tap on the door. Pause. Another tap, louder. Pause.

FAITH (*off*). Mum.

Pause.

(*Off. Louder.*) Mum! The door's still locked.

Pause.

(*Off.*) Please let me in.

Pause.

(*Off.*) Please, Mum.

EVELYN. I am not coming out.

FAITH (*off*). You can't just stay in there.

EVELYN. Can I not?

FAITH (*off*). What about dinner?

EVELYN. Eat without me.

FAITH (*off*). What about tonight?

EVELYN. Leave me alone.

FAITH (*off*). This is crazy.

Pause.

(*Off.*) I'm sorry about what I said.

Pause.

(*Off.*) Mum? Can you still hear me?

EVELYN. Go away.

FAITH (*off*). I'm worried about you.

EVELYN. It's too late.

Pause.

FAITH (*off*). Mum.

EVELYN. I'm going to stop talking to you now.

FAITH (*off*). Shit!

Silence.

EVELYN. I didn't bring you up to speak as if your mouth were
filled with sewage.

A man's voice repeating 'Sieg Heil' is heard.

The POSTMAN *enters. He is frog-marching, making a
Hitler moustache on his upper lip with the index finger of
one hand and doing the Nazi salute with the other.*

POSTMAN. Sieg Heil! Sieg Heil! Sieg Heil! Sieg Heil!

POSTMAN *takes out a parcel.*

German parcel delivered in ze German style.

POSTMAN *clicks his heels together, stands to attention and holds out the parcel.*

Pretty convincing, eh?

EVA. German peoples not do the finger under the nose.

POSTMAN. But the moustache is the most important thing about him.

EVA. You do fun. German people not do fun.

POSTMAN. No. They wouldn't.

POSTMAN *marches without the moustache.*

What about the marching?

EVA. I not know how do marching.

POSTMAN. I thought everyone in Boche Land learnt to march. Children 'n all.

EVA. Only some. Hitler Jugend.

POSTMAN. What's that?

EVA. Children army. I not in it.

POSTMAN. They must've taught you to 'Sieg Heil'?

EVA. In school. Do this.

She stands to attention and salutes.

'Heil Hitler!'

POSTMAN. Have to do that a lot, did you?

EVA. Too much.

POSTMAN. Not very fond of Hitler are you?

EVA. He not a good man.

POSTMAN. Thought he'd done wonderful things for your country.

EVA. Not for my family.

POSTMAN. Did you ever see him though?

EVA. See Hitler?

POSTMAN. Did you?

EVA. One time.

POSTMAN. Went to one of them rallies was it?

EVA. Not rally. In Hamburg city. He in car. Me on street. Lots
    people. They shout very loud.

POSTMAN. Did he smell?

EVA. Smell?

POSTMAN. Everyone knows he smells. All Germans smell.
    Well-known fact.

EVA. Not me.

POSTMAN. That's coz you've been here a bit. It's started to fade.

EVA (*smelling herself*). Girls in school in Hamburg say I smell.

POSTMAN. That's not very nice of them.

EVA. Which smells more, German or Jew?

POSTMAN. Same difference, love.

EVA. Thank you for the parcel.

POSTMAN. Thank you for the lesson in saluting (*He salutes.*)
    Heil Hitler!

    EVA *watches*.

POSTMAN. Do it back. Heil Hitler!

EVA. Heil Hitler!

    POSTMAN *exits*.

    EVA *carefully unwraps the parcel*.

HELGA. To the very best daughter any parents could wish for.
    The jobs. The permits. Thank you.

EVA. It wasn't all me.

HELGA. You have opened the door to a new and hopeful life.

EVA. Mrs Miller did as much as I did.

HELGA. Not long now. And then all of us together again. As I promised.

EVA *takes out of the parcel the* Rattenfänger *book, a letter and a Haggadah for Passover.*

Your storybook. I know how much you like it.

EVA *opens the letter.*

I also enclose your Haggadah for Passover.

EVA. When is Passover?

HELGA. I hear that there are lots of Jews in Manchester.

EVA. Is it before or after Easter?

HELGA. It will be easy to celebrate seder night with some of them.

EVA. Maybe it's happened already.

HELGA. We will be having a small seder. Not like the big ones we used to have.

EVA. I can't ask Mrs Miller to do a seder.

HELGA. 'Why is this night different from all other nights?' What will we do without you to sing the questions for us? What is a seder without the presence of the youngest child?

EVA. She'd think it was silly.

HELGA. We have never been a very religious family, Eva. But this has to do with more than religion.

EVA. Next year when they're here. I'll do it then.

HELGA. The Passover story has special meaning for us.

EVA. Maybe I could just read the Haggadah to myself. Would that count?

HELGA. Remember how the Israelites had to endure hard labour.

EVA. Some of it's quite boring though.

HELGA. How every son was thrown into the Nile.

EVA. The ten plagues upon the Egyptians is good.

HELGA. And Moses led the Israelites out of slavery and the waves of the Red Sea parted to let them through.

EVA. And when all the Egyptians follow into the path between the waves and get drowned. They deserved it.

HELGA. We must tell the story not as if it was experienced only by our ancestors but as if it happened to us. Not legend but truth. 'This is what happened to ME when I came out of Egypt.' This is how we survived and this is how we survive.

EVA. When did there stop being miracles?

HELGA. And remember the four sons: the wise son, the bad son, the stupid son and the son who doesn't even know what to ask. Try to be like the wise son, Eva.

EVA. What if I can't be wise?

HELGA. The weather here is lovely at the moment. The garden is looking beautiful. I wish I could bring it all with me over to England.

EVA. Will I get led like the Egyptians into the sea and drown forever?

HELGA. I am so looking forward to seeing you again and meeting your lovely English family. All my love. Mutti.

Banging on the door.

LIL (*off*). Let me in, Evelyn. I won't go away until you do.

EVELYN. Let me be.

LIL (*off*). You've had far too much time to be. That's enough.

EVELYN. Please go away, Mum.

LIL (*off*). I'll call the fire brigade if I have to. I'll say that the door's jammed . . .

EVELYN. No!

LIL (*off*). I will!

EVELYN. Go away.

LIL (*off*). I'll go and phone them now if you like.

> EVELYN *goes to the door. She unlocks it.* LIL *enters.*

I gave her hell.

> EVELYN *is silent.*

The state of this place.

> EVELYN *closes the door and locks it behind* LIL.

Now what are you doing?

EVELYN. I don't want anyone coming in.

LIL. There's no point locking the safe after the robber's been and gone.

EVELYN. I have to work out what to do.

LIL. How about airing this room for starters.

> EVELYN *lights up a cigarette. She offers one to* LIL.

I'm not meant to.

EVELYN. Just one. Keep me company.

LIL. I thought you'd given up.

EVELYN. I have.

> LIL *takes one and* EVELYN *lights it up.*

LIL. She didn't mean what she said.

EVELYN. She meant it.

LIL. It's probably still leftovers from her dad going. You're here to blame.

EVELYN. This has got nothing to do with her father.

LIL. She's always been hyper-sensitive.

> EVELYN *inhales deeply.*

I don't understand you.

EVELYN. Thought you knew me better than I know myself.

LIL. Not when you behave like this, I don't.

EVELYN. You think I'm paranoid too, do you?

LIL. I do at the moment.

EVELYN. Do you think I'm stiff as well?

LIL. You can be.

EVELYN. A terrible mother?

LIL. Not usually.

EVELYN. In what way am I being a terrible mother?

LIL. Locking her out when you should look her in the eye.

EVELYN. She hates me.

LIL. Why should she hate you? She's your daughter.

EVELYN. That's why she hates me.

LIL. Stuff and nonsense.

EVELYN. You heard the abuse she threw at me.

LIL. She was upset.

EVELYN. She'll never understand.

LIL. Let her get used to the idea.

EVELYN. She'll always blame me.

LIL. You've not done anything wrong.

EVELYN. We've all done something wrong.

LIL. Speak for yourself.

EVELYN. You told her.

LIL. She found those letters and photos and God knows what else. It didn't take a genius to put two and two together.

EVELYN. Who confirmed it?

LIL. What was I meant to do? Lie?

EVELYN. It is not necessary to lie.

LIL. You shouldn't have kept them.

EVELYN. That's not the point.

LIL. To be honest, Evelyn, I don't think it's such a big deal.

EVELYN. My daughter hates me and it's not a big deal?

LIL. You're the one who's making her hate you.

EVELYN. The whitewash has been stripped away and underneath is pure filth.

LIL. Now you're making no sense at all.

EVELYN. The more she knows, the worse it gets.

LIL. It was a long time ago. It doesn't matter any more.

EVELYN. Oh. It matters.

LIL. You'll put yourself over the edge if you're not careful.

EVELYN. Where else is there to go?

Sounds of children's chatter and train noises.

EVA very reluctantly puts a gas mask box on a string round her neck and picks up her small suitcase.

EVA. Will you visit me?

LIL. I said, didn't I.

EVA. And you tell Mutti and Vati how to find me when they come?

LIL. What did I say, Eva. Don't you trust me?

EVA. I have to be sure.

LIL. Have you got everything?

EVA. Teacher's already checked me.

LIL. Let me check you again.

EVA. Why?

LIL. Why'd you think? To be sure. What you got?

EVA. Bag.

LIL. Just one?

EVA. Yes.

LIL. Gas mask?

EVA. Yes.

LIL. Sandwiches?

EVA. Yes.

LIL. You're not wearing that jewellery are you?

EVA. I have to.

LIL. Anything could happen to it.

EVA. I'm not taking it off.

LIL. Give it me. I'll take it home . . .

EVA. I'm not taking it off.

Train whistle blows.

LIL. Better get a move on.

LIL *takes out a label.*

EVA. Why do I have to go now? There's no war.

LIL. It could start any time. All the children's going. We can tie it to your button hole.

EVA. Mummy Miller . . .

LIL. Where shall we put it then?

EVA. I saw someone on the platform.

LIL. Who?

EVA. He's coming to get me.

LIL. Who is?

EVA. He's waiting in the shadows.

LIL. There's no one there.

EVA. Don't make me go.

LIL. Nora and Margaret's going with their classes aren't they? It's not just you being evacuated. All the children have got to go. You'll be a heck of a lot safer out of the city. Keep still now. I can't get a grip.

EVA (*looking around*). Let me go tomorrow.

LIL. I said. There could be war any day. D'you want to be bombed to bits, gassed till you choke?

EVA. I might never come back.

LIL. It's my job to care about what happens to you, even if you don't.

EVA. But . . .

LIL. No buts. I want you safe and out of it.

EVA. But what about you and Uncle Jack?

LIL. Don't you worry about us.

EVA. But I do.

LIL. You'll thank me one day. (*Finishing the label.*) It's on! Right . . . Bye bye, lovie . . .

They hug. EVA *clings on.*

Let go now.

EVA. Don't want to.

LIL *pulls herself away from* EVA *and puts her on the train.*

LIL. It's for your own good.

EVA. I'd rather get bombed.

LIL. I'll visit you at the weekend.

EVA *looks very miserable and starts to wave.*

Whistle blows again.

Sounds of train about to start to move.

EVA. We've got to stop! He'll take us over the edge. Got to get away from him. (*She starts to choke and cough.*)

EVELYN *starts coughing.*

Sounds of train moving.

This can't happen! It mustn't happen! Help! Leave me alone! Leave me alone! Help!

EVA *leaps and lands with a roll, then lies still.*

LIL (*off*). Eva! Eva Schlesinger!

EVA *raises her head. She is dazed.*

EVA. Am I in the abyss?

LIL. You're with me.

EVA. Did I get away?

LIL. And how.

EVA. Has the Ratcatcher gone?

LIL. There's no one here.

EVA. Are you sure?

LIL. I'm sure.

EVA. He didn't get me.

LIL. Have you broken anything?

EVA (*sitting up slowly*). Don't think so.

LIL. You didn't hit your head.

EVA. Are you cross?

LIL. Cross! (*Realising she isn't.*) No. (*She pauses.*) I'm sorry.

EVA. You're sorry?

LIL. Should've realised. Shouldn't have made you go.

EVA. The ground was moving.

LIL. It isn't what you need most.

EVA. Couldn't keep my balance.

LIL (*helping* EVA *take off her gas mask*). I didn't want you to go. More than Margaret and Nora. Don't know why.

EVA. You didn't say.

LIL. Didn't want to upset you. If I'd clung, you would've done. Can you get up?

EVA. Have I been very bad?

LIL. No. Eva. I'm the one who got it wrong.

LIL *helps* EVA *up.*

EVELYN. What shall I do with the papers?

LIL. You should've known she'd find them one day.

EVELYN. She's never searched in here in her life.

LIL. Burying's not enough, love. You have to get rid.

EVELYN. How could I get rid of them? There are documents in there that prove I have a right to be here. Papers that will stop them from sending me away.

LIL. Who'd want to send you away?

EVELYN. Someone. Anyone. You can never tell. Who knows what they may be thinking.

LIL. Who for God's sake!

EVELYN. The authorities.

LIL. Your passport's not in there is it?

EVELYN. Not my current one.

LIL. And your naturalisation papers?

EVELYN. The first entry permit is. There might be other documents.

LIL. Dig them out then.

EVELYN. I don't want to touch those letters and pictures.

LIL. I'll help.

EVELYN *pulls back.*

Don't you trust me?

EVELYN. Yes.

LIL. I'll sort them out with you.

LIL *brings the box of papers over and takes out a letter. She holds it out to* EVELYN.

Do you want to keep this?

EVELYN *looks at the letter.*

It's personal not official.

EVELYN. No.

LIL. What shall I do with it?

EVELYN (*taking it*). I'll rip it up.

EVELYN *holds it.*

LIL. If you're going to do it, do it.

EVELYN *is still.*

What're you waiting for? Get tearing.

EVELYN *looks at the paper.*

Go on.

EVELYN. Why are you so keen for me destroy everything?

LIL. I thought you wanted shut of it.

EVELYN. I do . . . I just . . .

LIL. Here love, let me.

EVELYN. No.

LIL. If you can't, I will.

EVELYN. It's mine not yours.

LIL. Don't be so daft.

EVELYN. You've always done too much.

LIL. How could I ever do enough?

EVELYN. You took too much.

LIL. How did I take?

EVELYN. Too much of me.

LIL. What d'you mean by that?

EVELYN. I wasn't your child.

LIL. As good as . . .

EVELYN. You made me betray her.

LIL. I got you through it. Never forget that, Evelyn.

EVELYN. You made me betray them.

LIL. I was with you and I put up with you and I stuck by you. That's what mothering's all about. Being there when it counts. No one else was there, were they? And good or bad, I'm still here. Who else have you got?

EVELYN. No one.

LIL. That's right, Evelyn, no one.

EVELYN. And isn't that what you always wanted?

LIL. Did I start the war? Am I Hitler?

EVELYN. You might as well have been.

LIL. What have I done to you that wasn't done in love?

EVELYN. What are you? Some saint? . . .

LIL. I didn't have to take you in . . .

EVELYN. Some saviour to all the world's poor little orphans?

LIL. I could've starved you or worked you . . .

EVELYN. And what do I have to pay?

LIL. I could've hit you . . .

EVELYN. What's your price?

LIL. I saved you.

EVELYN. Part of me is dead because of you.

LIL. Nothing you say will make me walk out that door.

EVELYN. Murderer.

LIL. I kept you alive. More than alive.

EVELYN. Child-stealer.

LIL. Go on then. Bare your grudges at me. What else do you want to blame me for? What other ills in your life are all down to me?

EVELYN. Shut up.

LIL. I'm waiting.

EVELYN. I don't want to blame you.

LIL. What do you want?

EVELYN. I want it never to have happened.

LIL. Well it did.

Pause.

Now what?

EVELYN. Enough.

EVELYN *tears up the letter into small pieces. She and* LIL *proceed to destroy each item in the box.*

STATION GUARD *enters.*

GUARD (*to* EVA). Can I help you, love?

EVA. What?

GUARD. You waiting for someone?

EVA. Two people.

GUARD. What do they look like, love?

EVA *takes out a photo and shows it.*

Well-heeled.

EVA. Mother knows a good cobbler.

GUARD. Right. Is that them?

EVA. No.

GUARD. They your parents are they?

EVA. Yes.

They look.

GUARD (*pointing*). What about those two?

EVA. No.

GUARD. You're not here on your own to meet them are you?

EVA. Mrs Miller has just gone to cloakroom.

GUARD. Who's that then?

EVA. She looks after me.

GUARD. She knows where to find you?

EVA. Oh yes.

GUARD. Live in Manchester do you?

EVA. Yes.

GUARD. Not been evacuated then?

EVA. No.

They look.

GUARD. Well, I'm afraid they don't seem to be here, your Mam and Dad.

EVA. They will come.

GUARD. You sure they were on this train?

EVA. They write that they come to me on September 9th.

GUARD. But, it's September 11th today.

EVA. They must to come soon.

GUARD. Look. Are you certain they were travelling from London?

EVA. Yes . . . it must be . . . I got here from there.

GUARD. You see there's no more trains today from London.

EVA. Are you sure?

GUARD. Course I am.

EVA. It can't be.

GUARD (*suspicious*). Where are you from?

EVA. 72 Mulberry Road . . .

GUARD. No. I mean, what's your nationality?

EVA. My?

GUARD. What country you from?

EVA (*worried*). I don't live there any more.

GUARD. Where don't you live any more?

EVA. It does not matter so much.

GUARD. And where's this lady who's looking after you?
     She's left you a long time on your own hasn't she?

EVA. I don't know.

GUARD (*taking her by the arm*). I think that you'd better
     come with me young lady.

     LIL *runs up to* EVA.

LIL. Eva! Eva! Where the hell did you go!

GUARD. Are you supposed to be looking after her?

LIL. I just went to the cloakroom.

GUARD. You should take better care of her. Can't leave a girl
     of her age on her own. Specially nowadays. Could be an air
     raid warning any minute.

LIL. She ran off. (*To* EVA.) What d'you do that for? You had
     me frantic. D'you think I like pacing platforms looking for
     you!

GUARD. And what's this about her being a foreigner?

LIL (*to* EVA). The last train's been and gone, love.

EVA. We cannot to give up yet.

LIL. We've been here three days on the trot.

EVA. Please can we come back tomorrow.

LIL. I don't think they're coming. (*To* GUARD.) I'll take her now.

GUARD. I asked you about her being a foreigner?

LIL (*to* GUARD). Don't worry yourself about it.

GUARD. Got to look out for spies we have.

LIL. She's not a spy. She's ten years old.

GUARD. What about them parents she's waiting for?

LIL. Her parents are still in Germany.

EVA. No, they're not!

GUARD. Are they indeed?

LIL. Just leave it to me, will you. (*To* EVA.) I did warn you that this would happen.

GUARD. What's she doing here then? She should be in Germany with them.

EVA. Maybe they're in London.

LIL. Eva. They're not coming.

EVA. They keep their promises. Always.

LIL. Wars break promises.

EVA. They must be coming some different way. They have their visas got by now . . . they have written to us that they come this week . . .

LIL. They wrote that before the war started. If it'd broke out a fortnight later . . .

EVA. I want them to come. I got permits!

LIL. Believe me, Eva love, I want them to come too.

GUARD. Well, I don't.

EVA. You are wrong! You are wrong! They will come!

LIL. There's no way through.

EVA. There is!

LIL. There isn't.

GUARD. If they put one foot into this country, they'll be interned straight off. Got to protect ourselves.

EVA. No!

LIL. Oh Eva.

EVA. No! No! No! No! No!

LIL. I know. I know.

EVA. No!

>   EVA *shakes with distress*.

GUARD (*exiting*). Should've stayed where she belongs.

LIL. We can go to church and pray for them.

EVA. I'll never see them again, will I?

LIL. They've got as much chance of surviving as we have. And I'm not dying and neither are you.

>   EVA *takes off two rings, a charm bracelet, a watch and a chain with a Star of David on it*.

What're you doing?

EVA. I don't want these on me any more.

LIL. Why on earth not?

EVA. I don't like them.

LIL. We'll put them away safe at home.

EVA. How much longer can I stay with you?

LIL. Don't ask stupid questions.

>   LIL *takes* EVA*'s arm*. EVA *slowly moves with her*.

>   EVELYN *rips*. LIL *picks up the* Rattenfänger *book and starts to tear out the first page*.

EVELYN. No. Not that.

LIL. It's in German. Horrible pictures.

EVELYN. You can't damage a book. I'll give it to a second hand shop.

LIL (*picking up the Haggadah*). What about this?

EVELYN. That too.

EVELYN *puts the books to the side.* LIL *opens a letter.*

EVELYN *picks up the mouth organ. She doesn't recognise it. She puts it with the books.*

LIL *reads the letter in her hand intently.*

EVELYN. Is it important?

LIL. It's them changing their mind about letting you stay on at school after we fought them . . .

EVELYN. Rip it up.

LIL. 'We accept Eva's proven brilliancy . . . '

EVELYN. Mum.

LIL. Can't we save it?

EVELYN. What did you say about destroying?

LIL *witholds it.*

You were absolutely right. All this unpleasantness could have been avoided. I should have sifted through all these years ago. It's only paper.

LIL. I suppose.

EVELYN. What's done is done, Mum.

EVELYN *takes the letter and tears it.*

Let's get back to normal shall we?

LIL. You've got over worse.

EVELYN. I've made a good life. All I can do is live it and count my blessings.

LIL. And make up with your daughter.

EVELYN. We'll see.

LIL. You always have to make an effort with your children. No matter what.

EVELYN. All our children leave us. And one day they never come back. I can't stop her.

LIL. You and I are still close.

EVELYN. You and I are different.

LIL. She's more like you than you think.

EVELYN. I don't want her to be like me.

LIL. She's herself too. Every child's their own person.

EVELYN. Was I?

LIL. And how.

EVELYN. Not any more. The older I get the less of myself I become.

LIL. The things you come out with.

EVELYN. I always knew she'd go. Didn't the German woman realise that too?

LIL. You mean your first mother?

EVELYN. She wanted me to be hers forever.

LIL. I thought you'd forgotten her.

EVELYN. It doesn't matter. I have.

   EVELYN *continues to tear.*

   Soundtrack of a newsreel about the liberation of Belsen.

   LIL *and* EVA (*now fifteen*) *watch. Suddenly* LIL *puts her hands over* EVA*'s eyes and bundles her away.*

LIL. They should have a warning about what's in them newsreels. No children should see such pictures.

EVA (*pushing away* LIL*'s hands*). I'm not a child. I'm fifteen.

LIL. Especially not you. No matter how old you are.

EVA. It can't be kept from me forever.

LIL. D'you want to go back in then?

Pause.

EVA. No.

EVA. The soldiers had handkerchiefs over their noses and mouths.

LIL. Don't think of it.

EVA. Can a handkerchief keep out the smell of all those bodies?

LIL. It couldn't hold all the tears that want crying.

Pause.

EVA. I don't want to cry.

LIL. Far too shocking.

EVA. Should I want to cry? Is it callous of me?

LIL. You react as you react.

EVA. We can still go in to see the main feature, can't we?

LIL. Do you want to?

EVA. Yes. Is that wrong?

LIL. It was our treat.

EVA. There's no reason why we should miss our treat is there? I mean, it wouldn't make any difference to anything else would it?

LIL. Sure you're in the mood?

EVA. I have been looking forward to it.

LIL. I don't know if I'm in the mood now.

EVA. You've already paid for the tickets and we won't have another chance before it finishes.

LIL. Alright.

Knocking on the door.

FAITH (*off*). Gran? Mum?

EVELYN *shakes her head*.

LIL. Go on down, Faith, love.

FAITH (*off*). What are you doing?

LIL. Let me sort it out.

FAITH (*off*). Let me in.

LIL. We'll be out soon. Promise.

FAITH (*off*). How soon?

LIL. Not long.

FAITH (*off*). I'll wait here.

EVA *stands on a box*. LIL *starts to fix her skirt hem*.

EVA. Thank you for helping.

LIL (*to* EVA). You can do your own hem next time.

EVA. You know I'm no good at sewing.

LIL. You'll have to learn sooner or later.

EVA (*taking the gold watch and jewellery out of her pocket*). How much d'you think they're worth?

LIL. What's worth?

EVA. Two rings. A charm bracelet. Gold. A chain with a Star of David. A watch. All gold.

LIL. Don't ask me. I'm not a jeweller.

EVA. It'd be quite a lot, wouldn't it?

EVA *peers at the jewellery*.

LIL. Why d'you want to know?

EVA. I was thinking of selling them.

LIL. What d'you want to sell them for?

EVA. I'm fed up of hiding the watch under my socks to stop hearing the ticking at night.

LIL. It's bad luck to sell a keepsake.

EVA. I'd rather have the money.

LIL. Money's nothing. You purse it, you spend it. Those are more.

EVA. If they're mine, I can do what I want with them.

LIL. Are they yours?

EVA. My mother from Germany gave them to me.

LIL. To look after for her or have for yourself?

EVA. Same difference now.

LIL. We're still trying to track them down, aren't we? Still writing all those letters. Why are you so keen to give up?

EVA. It was all over a long time ago.

LIL. It isn't over till you know for sure.

EVA. I will sell them, Mum. There's better things the money could be spent on.

LIL. Like what?

EVA. I want to pay my way for myself as much as I can.

LIL. And I want to keep you. Like no one ever kept me. I don't care if it's hard. I'll do right by you. Somebody has to in this godforsaken world.

EVA. You've already done more than alright by me.

LIL. I've not finished yet.

EVA. D'you mind if I go now?

LIL. Just make sure no one diddles you.

Knocking on the door.

FAITH (*off*). Let me in. Please, let me in.

EVELYN *nods.* LIL *opens the door.* FAITH *enters.*

FAITH. My God.

EVELYN. We're going to clean this room up now.

FAITH. I didn't mean to shout at you like that.

EVELYN. It's over and done with.

FAITH. I'm sorry.

EVELYN. It's forgotten.

LIL *tidies around the box of torn papers.*

FAITH. What are those?

EVELYN. I've put an end to the trouble.

FAITH. You've torn up those letters and photos . . .

EVELYN. It's the only way forward.

FAITH (*to* LIL). How could you let her do this?

LIL. It's what we both think is best.

FAITH *kneels down and stares at the pieces. She tries to gather and fit them together.*

EVELYN. Don't get yourself all worked up now darling.

FAITH. Weren't these family documents . . . I mean . . . more than that . . .

EVELYN. I know what they were.

LIL (*to* EVELYN). No one's accusing you, love.

FAITH. But . . . weren't these things . . . sort of . . . entrusted to you? Why didn't you look after them?

EVELYN *is silent.*

Why didn't you pass them on to me?

EVELYN. I can do what I want with my own property.

FAITH. But how do I know what went before without them? How does anyone know? What proof is there? It could all be make-believe, couldn't it?

LIL (*to* FAITH). You're not doing a very good job of making up, Faith.

FAITH (*picking up scraps of paper from the floor*). Look at these remains. Where's the body for these feet? The hand for these fingers? Now they're just lost in the millions.

EVELYN. You know, Faith, there are hundreds of books on the subject. Read some of those if you must have a morbid interest in past events.

FAITH. Who's going to take care of their memory?

EVELYN. Are you going to go on at me about this for the rest of our lives?

FAITH. Did they die for you to forget?

EVELYN. Why are you being so cruel?

FAITH. Destroying these was crueller.

EVELYN. Do you think I don't know that.

FAITH. Why did you do it then?

EVELYN. Because – and I don't expect you to begin to understand this – it helps me? It gives me something I can do in the face of it all.

FAITH. It can't change what happened though, can it?

EVELYN. Do you want to draw blood?

FAITH. Not blood.

EVELYN. Well, blood is all I have left. Gallons and gallons of the freezing stuff stuck in my veins. One prick, Faith, and I might bleed forever.

FAITH. Mother, don't . . .

EVELYN. Do you still want to know about my childhood, about my origins, about my parents?

FAITH. Yes.

EVELYN. Well, let me tell you. Let me tell you what little remains in my brain. And if I do, will you leave me alone afterwards. Will you please leave me alone?

FAITH. If that's what you want.

EVELYN. My father was called Werner Schlesinger. My mother was called Helga. They lived in Hamburg. They were Jews. I was an only child. I think I must have loved them a lot at one time. One forgets what these things feel like. Other feelings displace the original ones. I remember a huge cone of sweets that I had on my first day at school. There were a lot of toffees . . .

FAITH. What else?

LIL. Faith.

FAITH. What else do you remember?

EVELYN. Books. Rows and rows . . . a whole house built of books and some of them were mine. A storybook filled with dreadful pictures: a terrifying man with razor eyes, long, long fingernails, hair like rats' tails who could see wherever you were, whatever you did, no matter how careful you tried to be, who could get in through sealed windows and closed doors . . .

FAITH. Go on.

EVELYN. The only other thing is a boy with a squint on the train I came away on. I kept trying not to look at him. Please believe me, Faith, there is nothing else in my memory from that time. It honestly is blank.

FAITH. What happened to your parents?

EVELYN. They died.

FAITH. In a concentration camp?

EVELYN. Yes. In Auschwitz.

LIL. When did you find that out?

FAITH. When did they die?

EVELYN. My father died in 1943. He was gassed soon after arrival.

FAITH. What about your mother?

EVELYN. My mother . . . she was . . . she was not gassed.

FAITH. What happened to her?

HELGA *enters. She is utterly transformed – thin, wizened, old-looking. Her hair is thin and short.*

HELGA. Ist das Eva? (*Is it Eva?*)

EVA *is speechless.*

HELGA. Bist Du das, Eva? (*Is that you, Eva?*)

EVA. Mother?

HELGA *approaches* EVA *and hugs her.* EVA *tries to hug back but is clearly very uncomfortable.*

HELGA. Ich hätte Dich nicht erkannt. (*How much you have changed.*)

EVA. I'm sorry. I don't quite understand.

HELGA. How much you have changed.

EVA. So have you.

HELGA. You are sixteen now.

EVA. Seventeen.

HELGA. Blue is suiting to you. A lovely dress.

EVA. Thank you.

HELGA. You are very pretty.

EVA. This is a nice hotel. I can't believe you're here.

HELGA. I promised I would come, Eva.

EVA. I'm called Evelyn now.

HELGA. What is Evelyn?

EVA. I changed my name.

HELGA. Why?

EVA. I wanted an English name.

HELGA. Eva was the name of your great grandmother.

EVA. I didn't mean any disrespect.

HELGA. No. Of course not.

EVA. I'm sorry.

HELGA. Nothing is the same any more.

EVA. It's just that I've settled down now.

HELGA. These are the pieces of my life.

EVA. There were no letters for all those years and then I saw the newsreels and newspapers . . .

HELGA. I am putting them all back together again.

EVA. I thought the worst.

HELGA. I always promised that I would come and get you.

EVA. I was a little girl then.

HELGA. I am sorry that there has been such a delay. It was not of my making. (*Pause.*) I am your Mutti, Eva.

EVA. Evelyn.

HELGA. Eva. Now I am here, you have back your proper name.

EVA. Evelyn is on my naturalisation papers.

HELGA. Naturalised as English?

EVA. And adopted by Mr and Mrs Miller.

HELGA. How can you be adopted when your own mother is alive for you?

EVA. I thought that you were not alive.

HELGA. Never mind it. We have all done bad things in the last years that we regret. That is how we survive.

EVA. What did you do?

HELGA. I was right to send you here, yes? It is good to survive. Is it not, Eva?

EVA. Please call me Evelyn.

HELGA. Now we must put our lives right again. We will go to New York where your Onkel Klaus will help us to make a beginning.

EVA. All the way to New York?

HELGA. Who is here for us? No one. The remains of our family is in America.

EVA. I have a family here.

HELGA. These people were just a help to you in bad times. You can to leave them now behind. The bad times are finished. I know it.

EVA. I like it here.

HELGA. You will like it better in America.

EVA. Do I have to go away with you?

HELGA. That is what I came for.

RATCATCHER *music*.

Scene Two

The torn papers and their box have been cleared away.

HELGA, *holding a suitcase, stands in a corner.*

EVELYN *has opened the box of glasses. She rubs one with a tea towel.*

FAITH *watches.*

EVELYN (*holding up a glass*). Will these be of any use?

FAITH. Aren't they a bit precious?

EVELYN. You can have them if you want them.

FAITH. If you're sure . . .

EVELYN. Yes or no?

FAITH. Yes.

EVELYN. Good. That's glasses done.

   FAITH *picks up the box and puts it by the door.*

   EVELYN *moves on to another box.*

   LIL *enters. She is wearing a coat.*

LIL. I'm off out now.

EVELYN. Will you be back for dinner?

LIL. Yes.

FAITH. Do you want me to give you a lift to the station tomorrow?

EVELYN. I said that I would.

FAITH. You hate driving into town.

LIL (*to* FAITH). I told her she didn't have to.

EVELYN (*to* LIL). I want to take you to the station.

LIL. You don't need to make anything up to me. I told you. It's alright.

EVELYN. Just let me take you.

LIL. Alright, take me.

EVELYN. I'll find out about departure times.

LIL. I've already got a timetable.

EVELYN. Fine.

LIL. See you later then.

EVELYN. See you later.

FAITH. Bye.

LIL *exits*.

FAITH *starts to search through some boxes*.

EVELYN. Don't you do a thing. You'll only cause a muddle. (*Opening a box*.) Do you need cutlery?

FAITH. What sort?

EVELYN (*pushing the box to her*). Look at it and decide.

FAITH. This is silver.

EVELYN. I don't like it.

FAITH. Why not?

EVELYN. The design's far too fussy.

FAITH. I like it.

EVELYN. Take it.

FAITH. Thanks.

EVELYN. Not at all.

FAITH *puts the box by the door*.

EVELYN *continues to check boxes*.

FAITH. Gran didn't know that your mother survived did she?

EVELYN. If she had known, she would have made me go with her.

FAITH. To New York?

EVELYN. She would have handed me back like a borrowed package.

FAITH. She might not.

EVELYN. You know your gran as well as I do, Faith.

FAITH. Did you ever see her after she left?

EVELYN. No.

FAITH. Was she still alive when I was born?

EVELYN. Yes.

FAITH. When did she die?

EVELYN. In 1969.

FAITH. She lived a long time.

EVELYN. She was a very strong woman.

FAITH. Didn't you ever want to be with her?

EVELYN. We didn't get on.

FAITH. You stopped me from knowing her.

EVELYN. I have tried to do my best for you. Please believe that.

FAITH. You stopped her from knowing me.

EVELYN. Don't hanker after the past. It's done.

FAITH. It's still a part of our lives.

EVELYN. It is an abyss.

FAITH. Before, all I knew was a blank space. Now, it's beginning to fill up. I have a background, a context.

EVELYN (*opening out two boxes*). Crockery?

FAITH (*looking at it*). It's beautiful.

EVELYN. A collection.

FAITH. Why don't you use it.

EVELYN. I prefer the Royal Crescent set downstairs. That's an old fancy. I've outgrown it.

FAITH. I'll probably break it all.

EVELYN. I hope you won't.

FAITH. I was joking.

EVELYN. Do you have enough storage space?

FAITH. There's lots of empty cupboards. (*Pause.*) Am I Jewish?

EVELYN. You've been baptized.

FAITH. Wouldn't the Nazis have said that I was?

EVELYN. You can't let people who hate you tell you what you are.

FAITH. I want to know what it means.

EVELYN. I'm afraid that I can't help.

FAITH. Don't you feel at all Jewish?

EVELYN. I was baptized when I was eighteen. I was cleansed that day. Purified.

FAITH. How can you say that?

EVELYN. I have been a great deal happier for it.

FAITH. What about being German?

EVELYN. Germany spat me out. England took me in. I love this place: the language, the countryside, the buildings, the sense of humour, even the food. I danced and sang when I got my first British passport. I was so proud of it. My certificate of belonging. You can't imagine what it was like.

FAITH. Why didn't you tell Dad?

EVELYN. Is it so wrong to want a decent, ordinary life?

FAITH. It's hard starting from scratch.

EVELYN. There's a portable television somewhere.

FAITH. This is what you're best at.

EVELYN. What is?

FAITH. Providing for me.

EVELYN (*pulling out a desk lamp*). What about a desk lamp?

FAITH. Does it work?

EVELYN. There's no bulb.

FAITH. That's no problem.

FAITH *turns to pick up a box.*

I'll start taking it all down.

EVELYN *pulls out the Haggadah and the* Rattenfänger *books.*

EVELYN (*holding them out to* FAITH). There are these too.

FAITH (*putting down the box*). You said everything had been destroyed.

EVELYN. They're just books. You might not want them . . .

FAITH (*taking the books*). Of course I want them.

EVELYN. One is the storybook and the other is for some Jewish festival.

FAITH. Thank you.

EVELYN *picks up the mouth organ.*

EVELYN. And this. It must have come with me.

FAITH *takes the mouth organ and lays it on top of a box.*

FAITH. I'd better start taking these down.

FAITH *picks up a box and starts to exit.*

EVELYN. Leave it to the left of the door in the hallway, not the right.

FAITH *exits.*

EVELYN *carefully sorts through boxes.*

Sounds of a quayside. A boat is about to leave.

EVA *enters.*

HELGA. Where have you been?

EVA. I said. In the lavatory.

HELGA. For half an hour in the lavatory?

EVA. I was being sick.

HELGA. Sick?

EVA. I'm alright now.

HELGA. Are you sure?

EVA. Yes.

HELGA. You should change your mind and come with me.

EVA. I haven't got a case.

HELGA. You could have your things sent on.

EVA. You said it was alright to come later.

HELGA. I said I would prefer you to come now. There is enough money from Onkel Klaus for a ticket.

EVA. I can't just leave.

HELGA. Why do you not want to be with your mother, Eva?

EVA. Evelyn. My name is Evelyn.

HELGA. Why are you so cold to me?

EVA. I don't mean to be cold.

HELGA. We have been together a week and you are still years away.

EVA. I can't help it.

Boat's hooter sounds.

HELGA. Boats do not wait for people.

EVA. I hope you have a safe trip.

HELGA. When is 'later' when you are coming?

EVA. In a month or two.

HELGA. Just get on the boat with me. Do it now.

EVA. I'm not ready yet. Not at all.

HELGA. You're making a mistake.

EVA. You're making me . . .

HELGA. What am I making you do! I am your mother. I love you. We must be together.

EVA. We've not been together for too long.

HELGA. That is why it is even more important now.

EVA. I can't leave home yet.

HELGA. Home is inside you. Inside me and you. It is not a place.

EVA. I don't understand what you mean.

HELGA. You are wasting a chance hardly anyone else has been given.

EVA. I will come.

HELGA. Will you?

EVA. If you want me to.

HELGA. If I want you to?

EVA. Just not yet.

HELGA. Do you want to come to make a new life with me?

EVA. You keep asking me that.

HELGA. Do you?

EVA. It's hard for me.

HELGA. I lost your father. He was sick and they put him in line for the showers. I saw it. You know what I say to you. I lost him. But I did not lose myself. Nearly, a million times over, right on the edge of life, but I held on. Why have you lost yourself, Eva?

Ship's horn sounds out.

I am going to start again. I want my daughter Eva with me. If you find her, Evelyn, by any chance, send her over to find me.

HELGA *embraces* EVA *who stands stock-still.*

HELGA *picks up her case and starts to walk away.*

EVELYN. Don't look at the razor eyes. Whatever you do.

She looks at HELGA.

Why do you only ever stare at me like that? Are those the only eyes you have? Didn't you have others once? I wish you had died.

HELGA. I wish you had lived.

EVELYN. I did my best.

HELGA. Hitler started the job and you finished it. You cut off my fingers and pulled out my hair one strand at a time.

EVELYN. You were the Ratcatcher. Those were his eyes, his face . . .

HELGA. You hung me out of the window by my ears and broke my soul into shreds.

EVELYN. You threw me into the sea with all your baggage on my shoulders.

HELGA. You can never excuse yourself.

EVELYN. How could I swim ashore with so much heaviness on me? I was drowning in leagues and leagues of salty water.

HELGA. I have bled oceans out of my eyes.

EVELYN. I had to let go to float.

HELGA. Snake. Slithering out of yourself like it was an unwanted skin. Worm.

EVELYN. What right have you got to accuse me? You kept saying something. What was it? Over and over? Yes. 'No,' you said. That was all. 'No. I won't help you. You have to be able to manage on your own. Take the needle. Sew the button and it's time to go. You don't need me. See. It's good.' Was it really so very good, Mutti? Was it really what you wanted?

HELGA. My suffering is monumental. Yours is personal.

EVA *exits*.

EVELYN. You should have hung onto me and never let me go.
Why did you send me away when you were in danger? No
one made you. You chose to do it. Didn't it ever occur to
you that I might have wanted to die with you. Because I
did. I never wanted to live without you and you made me.
What is more cruel than that? Except for coming back from
the dead and punishing me for surviving on my own.

EVELYN *sobs*. FAITH *enters*.

FAITH (*to* EVELYN). Are you crying?

FAITH *tries to get close to* EVELYN. EVELYN *does not
turn to face* FAITH.

What can I do for you? Please tell me what I can do to help?

EVELYN. Stay my little girl forever.

FAITH. I can't.

EVELYN. Then there's nothing you can do.

FAITH. I'm going to find out what everything means. Get in
touch with my relatives. I want to meet them.

EVELYN. You'll find them very different.

FAITH. I'm sure they'd love to see you too.

EVELYN. I have nothing in common with them and neither do
you.

FAITH. I want to put that right.

EVELYN. I don't want you to bring trouble onto yourself.

FAITH. There won't be any trouble.

EVELYN. You don't know . . .

FAITH. We can do this together. It would make us closer to
each other.

EVELYN. I'd rather die than go back.

FAITH. You might change your mind . . .

EVELYN. I can't.

HELGA *and* EVA *exit.*

FAITH. Can I have my toys?

EVELYN. Surely you can leave those here.

FAITH. I want to take them with me.

EVELYN. I'd like to keep something from when you were little.

FAITH. They mean a lot to me.

EVELYN. Take them.

FAITH *picks up the box of toys.*

Have you got everything you need now?

FAITH. More or less.

EVELYN. All done in here then.

FAITH. Yes we are.

FAITH *exits.*

The shadow of the RATCATCHER *covers the stage.*

The End.